THE BOOK OF REVELATION
MADE PLAIN AND CLEAR

FRANK L. THOMAS SR.

WESTBOW
PRESS®
A DIVISION OF THOMAS NELSON
& ZONDERVAN

This book is a work of non-fiction. Unless otherwise noted, the author and the publisher make no explicit guarantees as to the accuracy of the information contained in this book and in some cases, names of people and places have been altered to protect their privacy.

WestBow Press books may be ordered through booksellers or by contacting:

WestBow Press
A Division of Thomas Nelson & Zondervan
1663 Liberty Drive
Bloomington, IN 47403
www.westbowpress.com
1 (866) 928-1240

Because of the dynamic nature of the Internet, any web addresses or links contained in this book may have changed since publication and may no longer be valid. The views expressed in this work are solely those of the author and do not necessarily reflect the views of the publisher, and the publisher hereby disclaims any responsibility for them.

Any people depicted in stock imagery provided by Getty Images are models, and such images are being used for illustrative purposes only. Certain stock imagery © Getty Images.

ISBN: 978-1-9736-8724-5 (sc)
ISBN: 978-1-9736-8726-9 (hc)
ISBN: 978-1-9736-8725-2 (e)

Library of Congress Control Number: 2020903784

Print information available on the last page.

WestBow Press rev. date: 02/27/2020

THE BOOK OF REVELATION MADE PLAIN AND CLEAR

Frank L. Thomas
Sr. Pastor, Berean Calvary Chapel

Edited by Taylor Thomas
Forward by Joseph J. Marziale

A local church Pastor's simple, logical, straightforward
approach to the book of Revelation.

CONTENTS

Foreword xi

Introduction xv

Chapter 1   John on Patmos Vision of
glorified Jesus.................................... 1

Chapter 2   Smyrna and Philadelphia Receive
No Condemnation From Jesus;
Sardis and Laodicea Receive
Only Condemnation From Jesus 16

Chapter 3   Ephesus, Pergamos, and Thyatira
Receive Mixed Reviews From Jesus..... 23

Chapter 4   Vision of God's Throne 30

Chapter 5   The Slain Lamb of God is worthy
to take the Scroll............................... 36

Chapter 6   Seals 1-4: The Four Horsemen of
Man's History; The Fifth Seal:
The Souls Under The Altar and
The Rapture of The Church; The
Sixth Seal: Cosmic Disturbances/
Ezekiel Chapter 38 43

Chapter 7   144,000 Sealed Servants Raptured
             Church Seen In Heaven 65
Chapter 8   The Seventh Seal: The First 4
             Trumpets: The One-Third Judgments ... 83
Chapter 9   The Fifth & Sixth Trumpets:
             The Beginning of Woes 92
Chapter 10   The Mighty Angel and the Little
             Book 101
Chapter 11   The Two Witnesses and The
             Seventh Trumpet 106
Chapter 12   Woman With The Man Child,
             The Red Dragon, War In Heaven,
             Woman In The Wilderness 116
Chapter 13   The Last 3½ Years Begin;
             The Beast From the Sea and The
             Beast from the Earth 127
Chapter 14   3 Angels, 144,000 In Heaven,
             Christ Reaps The Harvest of the
             Tribulation Saints 137
Chapter 15   Seven Angels Given The Seven
             Last Judgments; Tribulation
             Saints Sing The Song of Moses 146
Chapter 16   The Seven Bowl Judgments 150
Chapter 17   Mystery Babylon The Great;
             The Scarlet Women Sitting on
             The Scarlet Beast 160
Chapter 18   The Fall of Babylon 170

Chapter 19   Marriage Supper of The Lamb
The Second Coming of Christ
The Battle of Armageddon 180

Chapter 20   Satan Is Bound, Millennial Reign
of Christ, Great White Throne of
Judgment 187

Chapter 21   New Heaven and New Earth and
The New Jerusalem 193

Chapter 22   The River of Life, The Warning,
Jesus Testifies To The Church 200

Works Cited 209

FOREWORD

It is my privilege to write the forward for this book. I would never have seen myself taking the position of doing that except that the Lord opened the door of opportunity in my life once again. Thank you to Pastor Thomas for writing this wonderful book and leading my church.

To write this forward, I must first read, and in reading, I must understand. I say that writing the forward for this book is my privilege because truly, beforehand, I had no understanding of the book of Revelation. I recall powering through it in seventh grade in a manner I like to call eyework: seeing the words on the pages, one by one, but never grasping the words' meanings in their book-long context. And still, right before Pastor Thomas offered me the opportunity of doing the forward for his book, Revelation was a mysterious text. Admittedly, and Pastor would nod me on this, some things in the Bible weren't meant to be known by man. But many Christians extrapolate this conviction onto the entire Revelation of Jesus Christ, ignoring it altogether. That approach may bring a sincere resolve to some, but truthfully it is dangerous to employ it. From a logical standpoint, this is my rebuttal: do you think the world is going to exist forever? If so, then you call God a liar, for much of the Word points to an earthly conclusion (Matthew 24:35, Hebrews 1:10-11, 2 Peter 3:10). If not, and if God has provided a book to man that prophecies the world's end, then why would He not intend for man to read it? It wasn't jotted down and preserved in vain. One may argue, "perhaps Revelation is included in the Bible because it is one of the inspirations of God, and so it must be included, lest something that God said was undocumented." To that I would respond with John 21:25 (KJV): "And there are also many other things which Jesus did, the which, if they should be written every one, I suppose that even the world itself could not contain the books that should be written. Amen." If the whole world wouldn't be able to contain the sum of God's works, and yet we have a Bible of roughly a thousand pages, then those thousand pages must be quite important; and if Revelation is a part of that small percentage which "made the cut," then surely it is worthy to be read. Therefore, give this book a try as I did. Don't fall into the same trap that many of those in my age group are subject to.

To give something of a personal testimony, all my life I have been surrounded by high school students like myself. While I fancy them as my friends and we laugh and enjoy each other's company, most of them do not concern themselves with the things of God. While most of them recognize themselves as Christians, the fruits of their lives are not indicative of a contrite heart before their God. I do not mean to say that they are innate mistake-makers and I am fresh of such offenses. Today I argue that like Paul, since I see the inner workings of my mind while I am yet silent, "This is a faithful saying, and worthy of all acceptation, that Christ Jesus came into the world to save sinners, of whom I am chief" (1 Timothy 1:15, KJV). Daily my mind conceives of foreign thoughts, many of which translate into action, all of which are unlike those of Jesus. However, the difference is that I continually repent from my contrary ways, while my friends do not feel the need to do so. I don't mean to generalize based on a small sample size, either. But, I see this trend of unchecked sin among the majority of people my age and social media. For those of you who are similar to me in age, be grateful that the Lord revealed Himself to you early. Don't worry about "missing out" on the failing pleasures of this life in which your secular friends may delve with happiness. Do not be fooled: "even in laughter the heart is sorrowful, and the end of that mirth is heaviness" (Psalm 14:13, KJV). Carry on. You are blameless in departing from that.

But do not be downcast that the world works this way! As Pastor Thomas will ensure you, this is all the Lord's plan. Actually, that's what Revelation is all about: the Good God whom we serve owns the timeline. And if all His words from Genesis to Jude have been proven right and trustworthy, you have every reason to trust in the prophecies found in Revelation. Another thing Pastor Thomas likes to say, "we are in the last days". Study His Word and watch it unfold around you. Continue in your eternal identity and let the Lord do His work in others and in you. Perhaps you are the medium He uses to bring someone to salvation. Non-believer, perhaps Pastor Thomas is that medium. Yet, as you extend yourself, do not rely on your own good, because there is none to be found. Remember Who provides it and kill the ego accordingly. C.S. Lewis says it better than me: "He loved us not because we were lovable, but because He is love." Hold onto that same attitude as you go through Revelation, and I pray it is your joy to do so.

I have no more to say! Enjoy the book!

Joseph J. Marziale

INTRODUCTION

As a local church Pastor I offer this thesis on the great book of Revelation from a heart of love for the flock Christ has called me to serve. I have written this thesis in the sincere hope that it may be of some aide to the reader in gaining further clarity and understanding of how near the return of our great God and King Jesus Christ is, and to be encouraged and strengthened in the days ahead. Let each of us always remember that all the victories have already been won in Jesus Christ before the foundation of the world. God's plan for creating man was that man may enjoy fellowship and communion with his Creator, and worship Him forever. *"Thou art worthy, O Lord, to receive glory and honor and power: for thou hast created all things, and for thy pleasure they are and were created,"* (Revelation 4:11). To know and love God however, is an individual choice. God Almighty created man with the capacity of free will choice; otherwise, the fall of man would have never occurred. We will speak more about this shortly.

It seems to me that over the years the great and

wonderful book of Revelation has been avoided by a great number of believers for several reasons. It has been my experience that many books written about the Revelation have tended to add to the confusion and misunderstanding about this fascinating book. Revelation is so wonderful in that it contains a special blessing for three groups of people: those who read it, those who hear it being read, and those who will take to heart and heed those things which are written! *"Blessed is he who reads and those who hear the words of this prophecy, and keep those things which are written in it; for the time is near" (Revelation 1:3).* Why is this book so important? We are told: because the time is near! Revelation is truly an exciting book!

It should be obvious to believers that our loving heavenly Father, *"who so loved the world that He gave His only begotten Son" (John 3:16)*, would never mean for the book, which was written to be the revelation of His Son Jesus Christ, to be complicated or confusing. His intent is never to frighten or confuse His children. Believers are clearly instructed that every book in the Bible is written for a very specific reason: to instruct, to comfort, and to bring hope! *"For whatever things were written before were written for our learning, that we through the patience and comfort of the Scriptures might have hope" (Romans 15:4-5).*

Pastor, teacher, and Bible expositor William R. Newell (1868-1956) had this to say regarding the book of Revelation, "I believe you scarcely need any commentary on this great book. The problem with men who come to Revelation and say it is difficult to understand, and impossible to interpret, is that they do not believe it. If you simply believe it and read it, it is very clear." To Pastor Newell's remarks, I would offer a hearty amen!

Most believers understand that the entire Word of God is God-breathed (2 Timothy 3:15-17) and points to Jesus Christ. Jesus said so himself in John 5:39, *"You study the Scriptures diligently because you think that in them you have eternal life; and these are they which testify of Me"* However, the book of the Revelation (in the Greek, *apokalupsis*; *unveiling*) of Jesus Christ is unique because it not only contains direct quotes of Jesus—but this book was personally dictated by Jesus! He used John, His scribe, to write to seven local churches regarding things which will take place in the last days of human history; the days, in fact, in which we ourselves are living today. That makes the book of Revelation of utmost importance and relevance to every believer to read, hear, and take heed for our instruction, for our comfort and to bring hope! And God our Father gave us this great book because He loves us!

As was mentioned earlier, at least one of God's purposes for creating man was that we would know God and enjoy fellowship with Him and worship Him.

Jeremiah recorded God's Word in Jeremiah 9:23-24, *"Thus says the Lord: 'Let not the wise man glory in his wisdom, Let not the mighty man glory in his might, nor let the rich man glory in his riches; But let him who glories glory in this, that he understands and knows Me, that I am the Lord, exercising lovingkindness, judgment, and righteousness in the earth. For in these I delight,' says the Lord."* God created man to know Him and to love Him. Love must be a free will choice or it is not love. Any expression of love or endearment which has been coerced or forced is not genuine and can never endure. God does not require our feigned affection.

We must understand that God did not create man to obey Him or do His bidding merely by rote repetition without processing it and understanding why. For this reason Adam and Eve were given a choice to make. The fact is that our loving Creator had informed them of what the results would be if they chose to eat of the tree of the knowledge of good and evil. The outcome of their choice was not something God "did to them" but was inherent in that particular action. Just as a loving parent warns their child of harmful or even deadly consequences of certain actions which they might make, such as putting their finger in a light socket, or running out onto a busy street, so our loving Creator has informed us of the results of actions which are contrary to His word.

If we are to understand the book of Revelation we must understand that God wants man to know Him, understand Him, and to be a participant in His program for planet Earth. Perhaps one of the best examples of this is found in Genesis 2:19-20 and 28-29 where He has Adam name the animals. Also found in Genesis 18:17 is the account of when the Lord met with Abraham, *"and the Lord said, 'Shall I hide from Abraham what I am doing?'"* God did not wish for Abraham to be unaware of His impending judgment upon Sodom and Gomorrah (Genesis 18:17), even though Abraham himself was not going to be subject to that judgment. Likewise, even though His Church, which is His Bride (John 3:29, Rev.21:9 and 22:17), will not be subject to God's wrath, which is coming upon the whole earth. He does not wish for His Church to be unaware (or misinformed) concerning the impending judgment that is coming upon an unbelieving, unrepentant world. Jesus gave us very specific signs to watch for so that we wouldn't be caught by surprise in the last days. Which is why when Jesus comes to take His Church out of this world before His judgment, believers will be watching and waiting! *"Looking for the blessed hope and glorious appearing of our great God and Savior Jesus Christ,"* (Titus 2:13); *"But you, brethren, are not in darkness, so that this Day should overtake you as a thief. You are all sons of light and sons of the day. We are not of the night nor of darkness. Therefore let us not sleep, as others do, but let us watch and be sober,"* (1 Thessalonians 5:4-6); *"Christ was sacrificed once to take away the sins of many people; and he will appear a second time, not to bear sin, but to bring salvation to those who are waiting for him,"* (Hebrews 9:28, NIV). *"They tell how you turned to God from idols to serve the living and true God, and to wait for his Son from heaven, whom he raised from the dead—Jesus, who rescues us from the coming wrath,"* (1 Thessalonians 1:9-10, NIV). *"Now there is in store for me the crown of righteousness, which the Lord, the righteous Judge, will award to me on that day—and not only to me, but also to all who have longed for his appearing,"* (2 Timothy 4:8).

Jesus sent this message to the Church to encourage not only those who are fully devoted to Him, such as those believers in the Church of Smyrna (Revelation 2:8-11) and the Church of Philadelphia (Revelation 3:7-13), for whom Jesus had no condemnation or correction—but also to encourage all those who had grown lukewarm to repent and become fully committed to the One who was and is fully committed to them. We can only love Him because He first loved us (1 John 4:19).

One of the important reasons for believers to study this book is so that they may not be caught unaware as the unbeliever will be. The Word of God encourages us in 1 Thessalonians 5:4-6 that we are to be children of the light, ready for and watching for our Redeemer. Jesus gave us the clearest clues so that we may not be caught unaware when He said, *"But as the days of Noah were, so also will the coming of the Son of Man be. But know this, that if the master of the house had known what hour the thief would come, he would have watched and not allowed his house to be broken into. Therefore you also be ready..."* (Matthew 24:37,43,44). Jesus' charge to *watch* can be found in Matthew 24:42 and 25:1, Mark 13:33,35, and 37, Luke 12:38 and 21:36, and finally in Revelation 3:3, *"Remember therefore how you have received and heard; hold fast and repent. Therefore if you will not watch, I will come upon you as a thief, and you will not know what hour I will come upon you."*

The Revelation of Jesus Christ was given to John the Apostle while he was imprisoned on the island of Patmos for his faith in Jesus. The purpose of this revelation was to encourage believers throughout the ages to persevere in the faith, no matter what time in history, circumstances, and or situation they find themselves. The Word of God opens with these words: *in the beginning.* We understand that if there was a beginning, then it follows that there must also be an end. The book of Revelation is the divine record of that end, and so believers are to be encouraged and instructed that our Sovereign God has His plan and order for human history well in hand, and that those who will experience the Tribulation might be informed and prepared for the greatest deception in human history which is coming upon the earth. This deception will be Satan's most potent in terms of both its scope and its effectiveness. Satan knows that he has but a short time left to accomplish his futile goal to be worshiped as God and to try to show God to be a liar who doesn't keep His promises (Revelation 12:12).

This last deception will be perpetrated by Satan, the False Prophet, and the Antichrist, a group of entities which work in concert together, and who collectively have been referred to as the "unholy trinity." We will deal with this group later on in the book. Keep in mind that the Word informs us that the purpose and function of biblical prophecy—proclaiming what is going to happen in advance—is that when it does come to pass, believers may be strengthened and encouraged in the faith. In John 13:19 Jesus said, *"Now I tell you before it comes, that when it does come to pass, you may believe that I am He."* Read also Isaiah 46:8-10 and 42:9.

Except for a very small portion in the beginning, the book of Revelation speaks almost entirely to what is yet to come. How unfortunate that many in the Church of Jesus Christ have been dissuaded, intimidated, and discouraged from doing a careful personal study of Revelation because, they were led to believe it could only be understood by the greatest biblical scholars.

This is only a book of dread to the one who refuses to believe God's Word as being truly holy and wholly true. But to believers it is a promise of being with our Lord while we escape all that is coming upon the face of the earth. I view Revelation differently from most, in that I believe this great book flows steadily forward in chronological order and does not require the reader to discern where it is necessary to jump back and forth throughout the book to rightly understand what is being revealed. I trust that as we progress through our study of the book of Revelation, the chronological flow will quickly become apparent to the reader.

The Prophet Daniel was shown that the tribulation period would last seven years. This seven-year period is the last "week of years" which has been determined for the Jews by God as described by Daniel in Daniel 9:24. As we study Revelation, we will find there are two distinct time signatures given. These two time signatures divide that last "week" which God revealed to Daniel, a seven-year period, into two 3½ year periods.

The first 3½ years, as first referred to in Revelation 11:3, is when two witnesses preach, (Keep in mind: the Jewish year is 360 days). The second 3½ year period is the final segment of the "last week" (Revelation 12:6) when Israel is divinely protected in the wilderness, and which closes out the period of time which is called, "the Tribulation". Another minor detail in which my view may differ from the traditional one is that I believe the entire last seven years of human history, as detailed in the book of Revelation, is simply the tribulation period. In Matthew 24:9-31 Jesus describes events which will occur during the tribulation period, and in verse 21 He adds the qualifying detail that since the beginning of the world until that time there has never been anything equal to it, referring to the seven year period which is laid out in detail in the Book of Revelation. Jesus is not telling His disciples that the tribulation is divided into two parts - "regular" tribulation and "great" tribulation. His point was to emphasize the sobering thought that even the globally devastating Flood judgment couldn't compare with that which is coming upon planet Earth!

Most Bible scholars agree that according to Daniel 9, there is going to be a seven-year period when the Lord God is once again going to use the Jews as His primary instruments for ministry and as His witnesses to the world. For the past two millennia, the Church of Jesus Christ has been the Lord's agent to represent Him and His program to the world, please read the letter to the Ephesians. Twice the Word of God refers to "the fullness of the Gentiles" having come in, and in Luke 21:24, the times of the Gentiles being "fulfilled." I believe these portions of God's Word speak to the fact that the Church will be absent and the Jews will once again be God's primary agents in the world. The 144,000 servants of God are also described in Revelation 14:4-5 as those who "follow the Lamb." Only believers serve God and follow the Lamb. Furthermore, in Revelation 7:3 the four angels are instructed <u>not</u> to begin their work of judgment <u>until</u> the 144,000 Jewish are sealed with the seal of God. **This specific charge to the angels to postpone their work of judgment clearly shows that the Tribulation did not begin with the opening of the first seal in Revelation 6:1.**

I believe it is important to make a distinction between the terms *'end of the age'* and *'the last days'*. The last days <u>began</u> with Pentecost, and will <u>end</u> at the *end of the age*. In Acts 2:1-4 and Acts 2:16-17, the Apostle Peter declared that the prophecy of Joel 2:28-32, the inauguration of the "last days", <u>was being fulfilled before their very eyes</u>! And so we understand that the "last days" began with Pentecost. Also, we read in Hebrews 1:1-2, *"God, who at various times and in various ways spoke in time past to the fathers by the prophets, has in these last days spoken to us by His Son."* On the other hand the *'end of the age'* includes the rapture, the tribulation, the Second Coming, and the Judgement of the nations, all of which help usher in <u>the age to come</u> which is the Millennial Reign of Christ on earth. In Matthew 24:3 when Jesus' disciples asked Him what would be *the sign of His coming and the end of the age* - they were not asking about the rapture. So we understand that the "end of the age" refers to a very specific time period.

I believe we are very close to the time when God's wrath will be poured out. It is very important to understand that God's wrath must be preceded by what we call the Rapture. In Luke 21:29-33 and Matthew 24:37-42,44 we read: "*then He spoke to them a parable: 'Look at the fig tree, and all the trees. When they are already budding, you see and know for yourselves that summer is now near. So you also, when you see these things happening, know that the kingdom of God is near. Assuredly, I say to you, this generation will by no means pass away till all things take place. Heaven and earth will pass away, but My words will by no means pass away'... 'But as the days of Noah were, so also will the coming of the Son of Man be. For as in the days before the flood, they were eating and drinking, marrying and giving in marriage, until the day that Noah entered the ark, and did not know until the flood came and took them all away, so also will the coming of the Son of Man be. Then two men will be in the field: one will be taken and the other left. Two women will be grinding at the mill: one will be taken and the other left. Watch therefore...that you also be ready.'*"

There is no doubt that we are in the last of the last days and are quickly approaching the end of this age. I believe that the Rapture: the calling-out of the Church is closer than most realize. This world is unraveling fast and there is no mending it.

The collection of nations currently assembled in Syria is a fulfillment of prophecy! I believe that the upcoming pullout of US troops will embolden Russia, Iran, and Turkey to continue aligning with other nations, mentioned in the prophecy of Ezekiel 38, to come against Israel from the north. What we see in Syria is a ticking time bomb that is ready to go off any moment. To deny or question that the fulfillment Ezekiel 38 is right on the horizon seems quite naïve. The hope we have from Scripture is that prior to that event, or perhaps at the same moment, the church of Jesus Christ is going to be raptured to meet Him in the clouds.

When we study the events which will occur after the rapture it's easy to think that they are irrelevant to us right now however, that is not the case. To see such future prophecies taking shape and coming into full focus before our eyes should encourage us to be more effective witnesses for Christ, and to have a sense of urgency to sound a warning to those who are not born again and are not going to be raptured with the church. Consequently, those who remain will live to experience the judgments described in the book of Revelation. We must keep our eyes on the Lord and lift up our heads because Jesus could be coming back for His Church any moment (Hebrews 12:1-2; Luke 21:28).

And so, our hope and our prayer is that this study will be a great encouragement to all believers to dive into the study of Revelation with earnest. For those of us living in such a time as this, the book of Revelation is quickly to become a book on current events!

REVELATION MADE PLAIN AND CLEAR TIME LINE

Chapter 1	Chapter 2	Chapter 3	Chapter 4	Chapter 5	Chapter 6	Chapter 7	Chapter 8	Chapter 9	Chapter 10	Chapter 11
	Letters to the 7 Churches						First 3½ years begins Trumpet Judgments			
John on Patmos	No Condemnation: Smyrna & Philadelphia	Mixed Reviews: Ephesus, Pergamos, and Thyatira	Vision of God's Throne	The Slain Lamb is worthy to take the scroll and to open the Seven Seals	Seals 1-4 The Four Horsemen of Mankind's History	Sealing Of the 144,000	7th Seal: Silence in Heaven for ½ Hour	Trumpets 5 & 6: Bottomless Pit Sun & air Darkened	The Mighty Angel and the Little Book	The Two Witnesses (2nd Woe past)
Vision of Glorified Jesus	Only Condemnation: Sardis & Laodicea				5th Seal: Souls Under The Altar and The RAPTURE	Great Multitude of Raptured Saints	Trumpets 1-4: The One-Third Judgments	200 million locust army	Seven Thunders	7th Trumpet The Kingdom of God proclaimed Temple of God Opened in Heaven (3rd Woe past)
					6th Seal: The War of Ezek 38			1/3 of man-kind killed (1st Woe past)		

Chapter 12	Chapter 13	Chapter 14	Chapter 15	Chapter 16	Chapter 17	Chapter 18	Chapter 19	Chapter 20	Chapter 21	Chapter 22
Woman with Man Child Red Dragon	Last 3½ years begins	3 Angels	7 Angels given the seven last plagues to complete the wrath of God	7 Bowl Judgments Begin: ①Sores ②Seas ③Rivers ④Sun ⑤Darkness ⑥Earthquake ⑦Hail	MYSTERY BABYLON THE GREAT	THE FALL OF BABYLON	MARRIAGE SUPPER OF THE LAMB	SATAN BOUND	ALL THINGS MADE NEW	The RIVER OF LIFE: Eternity With Jesus
	Beast from the Sea 7 heads, 10 horns, one blasphemous name	144,00 in Heaven	Tribulation Saints who had victory over the beast sing the song of Moses and the song of the Lamb		Scarlet Woman Sitting on the Scarlet Beast		SECOND COMING OF CHRIST	MILLENIAL REIGN OF CHRIST	The NEW HEAVEN And The NEW EARTH	WARNING
War in Heaven (Satan cast out)										
Woman in the Wilderness	Beast from the Earth (horns like a lamb, speaks like a dragon)	Christ Reaps the Harvest of Tribulation Saints					THE BATTLE OF ARMAGEDDON	GREAT WHITE THRONE JUDGMENT	The NEW JERUSALEM	JESUS' TESTIMO-NEY TO THE CHURCH

CHAPTER 1

JOHN ON PATMOS
VISION OF GLORIFIED JESUS

Rev 1:1-3: *"The Revelation of Jesus Christ, which God gave Him to show His servants — things which must shortly take place. And He sent and signified it by His angel to His servant John, who bore witness to the word of God, and to the testimony of Jesus Christ, to all things that he saw. Blessed is he who reads and those who hear the words of this prophecy, and keep those things which are written in it; for the time is near."*

Chapter one verse 1 opens immediately by informing the reader that this Revelation of Jesus Christ was given to Jesus by God the Father! Although the Revelation was dictated to the Apostle John two millennia ago yet it is clear that it was intended for the whole church throughout the Church Age—from its onset to the end of the church age—for both pre-tribulation and tribulation saints. This epistle was considered so necessary and important that God gave a promise to all who read and hear it. Then Jesus makes it clear that when He comes for His church in the clouds, distinguished from His second coming to earth when His foot touches the Mount of Olives and it splits in two, that every eye will see Him, both believers and unbelievers.

Rev.1:4-8: *"John to the seven churches which are in Asia: "Grace to you and peace from Him who is and who was and who is to come, and from the seven Spirits who are before His throne, and from Jesus Christ, the faithful witness, the firstborn from the dead, and the ruler over the kings of the earth. To Him who loved us and washed us from our sins in His own blood, and has made us kings and priests to His God and Father, to Him be glory and dominion forever and ever. Amen. Behold, He is coming with clouds, and every eye will see Him, even they who pierced Him. And all the tribes of the earth will mourn because of Him. Even so, Amen. I am the Alpha and the Omega, the Beginning and the End," says the Lord, "who is and who was and who is to come, the Almighty."*

We must remember that when the Rapture occurs Jesus comes *for* His Church to take them *out* of the world. In His Second Coming, He comes *with* His Church to establish His rule on earth. Due to the longstanding, traditional view of the Rapture being "secret" John's prophecy in 1:7 has been incorrectly applied to the *Second Coming* of Jesus rather than to the **Rapture of the Church,** which is the logical way to properly apply it. Consider that God's Word is not telling us that the Rapture is occurring at this point but merely is describing it for us. If the Rapture occurred at this point then the souls of martyred saints would not still be under the altar in chapter six.

Here is where misunderstanding the entire book of Revelation had its start. The Law of First Use is a theological term meaning that the way in which a portion of scripture is understood initially is the way it is always to be applied. The problem in this case is that a traditional understanding has been misapplied and so has distorted the entire flow of the book of Revelation. Here's what I mean: the mistaken idea of the Rapture being "secret" is based on 1 Corinthians 15:51-52, *"Behold, I tell you a mystery: We shall not all sleep, but we shall all be changed in a moment, in the twinkling of an eye* (1/10,000th of a second), *at the last trumpet. For the trumpet will sound, and the dead will be raised incorruptible, and we shall be changed."* But look closely, it does not say the *rapture* will take place in the twinkling of an eye, it says that **we are changed** in the twinkling of an eye. I can't find anywhere in scripture where it says the rapture will be secret but rather that it will be quite visible to all.

Let's now consider Acts 1:9-11, *"Now when He had spoken these things, while they watched, He was* *taken up, and a cloud received Him out of their sight. And while they looked steadfastly toward heaven <u>as He went up</u>, behold, two men stood by them in white apparel, who also said, 'Men of Galilee, why do you stand gazing up into heaven? This same Jesus, who was taken up from you into heaven, will so come in like manner <u>as you saw</u> Him go into heaven"* [emphasis added]. The clear reading of this verse indicates that in the same way that those present at the time of His Ascension watched Him ascend with their own eyes, so likewise in that same way He will be seen when He comes for His church. Jesus promised that His followers will not be on the earth for the Judgment (wrath) of God. Therefore, it follows that the angels' instructions are clearly referring to the rapture of the church. Believers will not merely be witnesses to Jesus' Second Coming to earth, they will be returning WITH Him. Clearly, the whole world will see Him coming "in like manner" because the rapture will not be "secret" but will be witnessed by one and all. Revelation 1:7, *"He is coming with clouds, and every eye will see Him, even they who pierced Him. And all the tribes of the earth* (referring to Rev.6:15-17) *will mourn because of Him."* The world will mourn because of the judgment that is coming. I trust that we have made clear the difference between the Rapture and the Second Coming.

Verse seven points out the eternal existence of Jesus Christ

He was in eternity past, is present with us now, and will be there in the end. I love the promise that we will be with Him for all eternity. For you and me as believers this is a wonderful promise which brings tremendous hope. Death is not the end for the believer but we will see our Lord face to face just as Job testified, *"And after my skin is destroyed, this I know, that in my flesh I shall see God, Whom I shall see for myself, and my eyes shall behold, and not another. How my heart yearns within me,"* (Job 19:26-27).

Vs.9-11: *"I, John, both your brother and companion in the tribulation and kingdom and patience of Jesus Christ, was on the island that is called Patmos for the word of God and for the testimony of Jesus Christ. I was in the Spirit on the Lord's Day, and I heard behind me a loud voice, as of a trumpet, saying, "I am the Alpha and the Omega, the First and the Last," and, "What you see, write in a book and send it to the seven churches which are in Asia: to Ephesus, to Smyrna, to Pergamos, to Thyatira, to Sardis, to Philadelphia, and to Laodicea."*

At verse nine John gives a personal testimony and discloses that this revelation was intended for all the church represented by seven churches that were located at that time off the Isle of Patmos. Notice that one of the first things John says is that he was in the

Spirit on the Lord's Day, the first day of the week also known for many years as the Christian Sabbath. The first day of the week is also referred to as the 8th day. God's covenant with Abram required that all males were to be circumcised on the 8th day after their birth. Jesus rose from the dead on the 8th day, the first day of the week, and the resurrected Jesus met with His disciples on the first day of the week as well (John 20:19). Many believers argue that whatever day of the week they choose to worship doesn't matter. First I pray all believers worship Him every day of the week. However I believe that the first day of the week was set aside by our Lord as the day which He ordained for His Church to gather to worship Him. The first day of the week, or 8th day, was set aside throughout Scripture as the day of special significance (Lev.12:2,3; 14:8-10; 15:13,14; 22:27, and Numbers 6:9,10). Most significant is that Jesus rose from the dead on the first day of the week. Just as God ordained the seventh day for the Jews to commemorate His completed work of creation because He rested on the seventh day, I believe that He has ordained the first day of the week for believers to celebrate Jesus' completed work of salvation and to worship Him.

A traditional teaching concerning the seven churches is that these are seven church ages that occur throughout history, and that we are now in the last church age of the Laodiceans. This view is neither logical nor is there scriptural support for it, but it is another example of the traditional approach to Revelation which renders it complicated and disjointed rather than flowing. Just using simple common sense we understand that all seven churches were present at the same time when John wrote this epistle, and all seven of these types of churches exist today.

Rev 1:12-16: *"Then I turned to see the voice that spoke with me. And having turned I saw seven golden lampstands, and in the midst of the seven lampstands One like the Son of Man, clothed with a garment down to the feet and girded about the chest with a golden band. His head and hair were white like wool, as white as snow, and His eyes like a flame of fire; His feet were like fine brass, as if refined in a furnace, and His voice as the sound of many waters; He had in His right hand seven stars, out of His mouth went a sharp two-edged sword, and His countenance was like the sun shining in its strength."*

John records for us the most amazing description of the risen and glorified Christ. What John sees is so glorious that he falls on his face in sheer adoration and worship. His eyes like a flame of fire indicates penetrating insight; He not only sees all, but He knows all. Given the limitations of human language this is the clearest description the Holy Spirit can convey of the glorified Jesus to His scribe, John. Daniel uses very similar phrasing to describe his vision of the pre-incarnate Christ in Daniel 10:5-6: *"I lifted my eyes and looked, and behold, a certain man clothed in linen, whose waist was girded with gold of Uphaz! His body was like beryl, his face like the appearance of lightning, his eyes like torches of fire, his arms and feet like burnished bronze in color, and the sound of his words like the voice of a multitude."*

Rev. 1:13 – *'One like the Son of Man'*: Jesus used this same term many times to identify Himself during His earthly ministry as did Daniel in the vision he was given of the reign of Jesus Christ in chapter seven and verses thirteen and fourteen.

A careful examination of the description of Jesus Christ given to us in Rev.1:13-16 helps us to better understand His offices of Prophet, Priest, and King:

1. Garment to the feet speaks of His total righteousness. All His acts are righteous (Revelation 19:8).

2. The golden band around His chest signifies His office as our eternal High Priest (the office of priest was that of mediator between man and God). Moses is given the specifications for the garments of the High Priest in Exodus 28:8 and 1 Tim 2:5 informs us: *"For there is one God and one Mediator between God and men, the Man Christ Jesus"*. The entire book of Hebrews

clearly establishes Jesus as our Great High Priest!

3. His head and hair were white like wool, as white as snow. White hair implies wisdom, and white garments imply purity. *Dan 7:9: "And the Ancient of Days* (indicating that He existed before time began; see also Isa.43:13) *was seated; his garment was white as snow, and the hair of His head was like pure wool."*

4. His feet were like fine brass, as if refined in a furnace. Brass is used in scripture of that which is firm, strong, and lasting. Gates of brass (Psalm 197:16); hoofs of brass (Micah 4:13); mountains of brass (Daniel 2:35); and many others. And, by implication of His strength, it also speaks of judgment.

5. His voice is as the sound of many waters. *Ezekiel 43:2 reads: And behold, the glory of the God of Israel came from the way of the east. His voice was like the sound of many waters; and the earth shone with His glory."* the voice of authority that drowns everything else out.

6. "He had in His right hand seven stars, out of His mouth went a sharp two-edged sword..." (Rev.1:16-17 and also 19:15 & 16). The seven stars will be explained in the next portion, but the sharp two-edged sword is defined by scripture. Eph 6:17 "[and] the sword of the Spirit, [which]

is the word of God"; In *Hebrews 4:12: "For the Word of God is living and powerful, and sharper than any two-edged sword, piercing even to the division of soul and spirit, and of joints and marrow, and is a discerner of the thoughts and intents of the heart."*

7. "...His countenance was like the sun shining in its strength" (Rev.1:17). John 1:4 and v. 9 we read, *"In Him was life, and the life was the light of men"*... *"that was the true Light which gives light to every man coming into the world."* Also, in Heb 1:3 we are instructed that God the Father has spoken through His Son, *"Who being the brightness of His glory and the express image of His person . . . is the image of the invisible God,"* and in Col.1:19, *"For it pleased the Father that in Him all the fullness should dwell."*

When we read this description of the resurrected glorified Jesus it should make us cringe at how He is portrayed not only by the world but even in many Christian educational materials. We have baby Jesus. We have European Jesus. We have effeminate Jesus. We have relevant Jesus. We even have claymation Jesus. I strongly believe that Children's Christian publications which depict any of the heroes of faith as confused, googled-eyed buffoons should be outright rejected.

Some might think this is not such a big deal, but it is; God does not need our help to make Jesus relatable. Heb. 13:8-9 informs us that, *"Jesus Christ is the same yesterday, today, and forever."* The absolute only way we may view God correctly is through the lens of God's Word! Anything else will give us a false image and thus impinge upon our relationship with Him. Jesus is not our good-old buddy, he is the risen and glorified King of Kings and Lord of Lords, our God and Savior who holds our salvation in the palm of His hands and in Him shines all the glory of the Godhead (Col.2:9 and Heb. 1:1-3). In addition, believers are admonished in 2 Cor. 5:16 not to regard Jesus as He was when He was here on earth, *"Even though we have known Christ according to the flesh, yet now we know Him thus no longer."*

Rev. 1:17-18: *"And when I saw Him, I fell at His feet as dead. But He laid His right hand on me, saying to me, "Do not be afraid; I am the First and the Last. I am He who lives, and was dead, and behold, I am alive forevermore. Amen. And I have the keys of Hades and of Death."*

Notice, John the beloved disciple didn't run up to Jesus and extend his hand, saying *"long time no see."* No, he fell down as a dead man. But notice Jesus' mercy and grace, *"He laid His right hand on me, saying to me, 'Do not be afraid.'"* This is the same right hand He has laid on us, telling us not to be afraid.

Psalm 27:1 assures the believer, *"The Lord is my light and my salvation; whom shall I fear? The Lord is the strength of my life; of whom shall I be afraid?"* [emphasis added]. He is the sacrificial lamb who took away the sin of the world, to all who call upon His Name, He died for our sins rising on the third day because death could not hold Him, and He is alive forevermore making continuous intercession for us. He alone holds our salvation in His hands, holding the keys to Hades, and Death. Surely, *"He who has the Son has life; he who does not have the Son of God does not have life"*. *"Whoever denies the Son does not have the Father either; he who acknowledges the Son has the Father also, I and My Father are one,"* (1John 5:12; 1John 2:23; John 10:30).

Rev.1:19-20: *"Do not be afraid; I am the First and the Last. I am He who lives, and was dead, and behold, I am alive forevermore. Amen. And I have the keys of Hades and of Death. Write the things which you have seen, and the things which are, and the things which will take place after this. The mystery of the seven stars which you saw in My right hand, and the seven golden lampstands: The seven stars are the angels of the seven churches, and the seven lampstands which you saw are the seven churches."*

The lampstands represent the church, which serves to give light to the people of this dark world. *"For you were once darkness, but now you are light in the*

Lord," (Eph. 5:8. See also Eph. 3:10-12; John 8:12; Acts 13:47). *"You are the light of the world. A city that is set on a hill cannot be hidden. Let your light so shine before men, that they may see your good works and glorify your Father in heaven"* (Matthew 5:14 &16).

At verse 20 of Revelation 1, Jesus reveals the mystery of the seven stars and the seven golden lampstands telling John that the seven stars are the seven angels, or *messengers,* of the seven churches which are located off the coast of Asia Minor. We understand that by the term "angel" Jesus is not meaning celestial angels but is rather referring to the pastor of each of the local churches mentioned by name. We know this because Jesus holds them personally accountable to obey His instructions. Hebrews 13:17 informs us that pastors will give an account for the flock that God has entrusted to them to feed and tend. Not all pastors are faithful to either God or His church, however celestial angels always do the Father's will (Ps. 103:20). On the other hand, Hebrews 1:14 informs us that all angels are ministering spirits sent to serve those who are saved, however they are not commissioned to lead local churches and are not the ones who will give account for said local church. Ephesians 4:11, 2 Timothy 4:2, and Acts 20:28 are a few portions which speak about the local church pastor's responsibility to the flock he has been called to serve. The call of God upon a man's life to pastor a local church is a very definite <u>call</u>, it is not a vocational choice. Church members who take special notice of their pastor's faults and shortcomings should be praying for him rather than calling into question his being led by the Holy Spirit. He is just a sinner who's been saved by grace just like they have; he has not arrived, but he has been *called* by God to feed His sheep. It is a very humbling and sobering position, because he will give an account to God. Most pastors have left much more lucrative positions and opportunities in order to answer God's call, and some have truly "left all" (Luke 5:11; Phil.3:7). And this is only one of the means by which God "proves" His call upon a man's life. The pastor who is truly called by God to feed and tend God's sheep must have no ulterior motives, no personal agenda. Otherwise, when the call becomes difficult and costly he will abandon the flock. In John 10:12-13 Jesus taught about the hired man who does not love the sheep and so when trouble comes will run away and leave the sheep. On the contrary, the man who has been called by God is not merely doing a job as a hireling. He has been called by God and is not feeding and tending God's flock for a salary. In fact, some men have walked away from financial security, benefits, and advancement more than once in faithful obedience to God's leading. Such a man has no other reason for doing what he is doing except to obey his Lord and to be faithful to God's call upon his life. Aside from a clear departure from

God's Word, church members need to think carefully before they take issue with their pastor's leadership. This is not referring to when a pastor departs from sound teaching or when his personal life no longer upholds the high standards for a pastor as outlined in 1 Tim. 3:1-3 and Titus 1:6-9. A faithful pastor is approachable and easy to talk to and will take the time to answer questions and will be patient and gentle. But when a church member calls into question their pastor's leadership just because they "don't agree with the direction the church is going", don't like his style of preaching, or approve of his level of education, they need to ask themselves whether perhaps they have been called by God to pastoral ministry, and whether or not they are willing to answer that call. If they have then they should leave all, follow God's call, and go plant a church.

CHAPTER 2

SMYRNA AND PHILADELPHIA RECEIVE
NO CONDEMNATION FROM JESUS;
SARDIS AND LAODICEA RECEIVE ONLY
CONDEMNATION FROM JESUS

The one and only cause, purpose, function, and clarion
call of the church of Jesus Christ is to worship Him in
spirit and in truth and to proclaim the gospel message.
In some cases a church and the people in it become
more enamored with church programs than they are
with Christ. Sadly, some have mistaken belief in
their doctrines and good works for belief in God. In
His letters to those churches to which He gives no
commendations Jesus addresses the sad occurrence
when a church becomes a finely tuned religious and
social organization, and has ceased to be a church.

There were more than seven churches in this
geographical area as recorded in Acts and the epistles.
The question is, why are *these* seven churches addressed
and only these seven? First, seven is the number of

completion or perfection, therefore, we can surmise that in these seven churches we have an example of the Universal Church past and present. I believe these seven churches were also selected because of their proximity to Patmos, and because in this group we see a perfect picture of what is pleasing to God and what is not.

As we study the letters to the churches I will not cover each church in detail, but lay out what I believe to be the important message Jesus gives to each church as it applies to us today. In each of the letters Jesus begins by assuring the true believers that He will come for His church before the Tribulation begins, at which time the ministry of God's program for planet Earth will once again be returned to the Jews; this period of time is also known as the seventieth week of Daniel as revealed in Daniel chapter nine.

Now, let's look at Jesus' letters to the seven churches. Two of the seven churches Jesus has no con*demn*ation for and two He has no com*men*dation for, and the other three churches have mixed reviews with both positive and negative issues addressed. As has been mentioned, these letters were written to the church—past, present, and future. Therefore, we can learn much from these letters as they apply to us today. Keep in mind that any church might be a combination of more than one of the seven churches, but this can also relate to us as individual Christians as well. Another thing to consider as we study these churches is that our faith is alive, and any believer can change some of the negatives mentioned by simply confessing to Jesus and repenting as per His instructions in Revelation 3:3.

It is important to take note that every one of the introductions to each of the seven churches contains a description of the glorified Lord Jesus, as was shown to John in chapter one. First let's look at the two churches which the Lord has only encouragement for. We find that neither of these two churches were large or wealthy churches. Rather, they were churches described as being persecuted and having little in resources. Clearly, great size and prominence is not necessarily an indication of God's approval.

SMYRNA: Rev 2:8-12

To the first church which receives no condemnation from Jesus is the church of Smyrna. Jesus makes reference to their tribulation and poverty, but makes it clear they were rich in faith. The Church of Smyrna is also encouraged by the Lord to not fear the things they were about to suffer by the hand of false believers (v.9). Jesus informs them that the devil himself will bring persecution, prison, and even testing on these true believers, but that persecution and testing will not be forever, and those who are faithful unto death receive the crown of life from the Lord Himself. We must always remember being a believer does not exempt us from difficult times, in fact we are told that testing is to be expected. *"Beloved, do not think it strange concerning the fiery trial which is to try you, as though some strange thing happened to you; but rejoice to the extent that you partake of Christ's sufferings, that when His glory is revealed, you may also be glad with exceeding joy,"* (1 Peter 4:12-13). Our hope and confidence is that even if we are to suffer in this life, we will not take part in the second death which is described in Rev.20:14 and 21.

PHILADELPHIA: Rev 3:7-13

To the church of Philadelphia Jesus makes it clear that He knows the work they are doing for Him and for the Kingdom of God. Jesus then makes the point of assuring them that even though they had little strength, were small, and poor, He has opened doors of ministry that no man can shut. The Lord encouraged them in the fact that they had kept His commands and had not denied His Name. Jesus also makes it clear that because of their faith in Him they would not take part in the Tribulation, but encourages them that He is coming quickly. Anyone who is not distracted by politics and takes a prophetic look at the world around us knows His coming is soon. For this reason we must hold fast to our faith. Jesus Himself has a crown for the believer that no one can take away. Jesus then promises the church of Philadelphia that they will be a pillar in the temple of God, and that the name of God and the new Jerusalem will be written on them, and they will have His New Name written on them as well. This can seem very confusing to many who read it, but it simply means God is going to seal us as being His for all eternity. I believe His New Name will be an understanding of His deity that we are unable to comprehend until we are with Him in glory.

SARDIS: Rev.3:1-6

Now, let's look at the churches Jesus had only condemnation for. The church of Sardis had a reputation for being an alive church, but they were dead in their faith and service to God. He even warns them that what life they have is ready to die. Jesus clarifies the reason He sees them as a dead church is because their activity and their works were not done out of love for Him. Church programs and good intentions and which are generated by the flesh do not require faith and so can never please God. Every operation of a Spirit led church will be by faith alone, not sharp marketing or organizational skills. For this reason Jesus tells them that He will come upon them as a thief, because they were too busy doing church stuff to be watching and longing for His appearing. Nevertheless, the Lord gives encouragement to those true believers who are in this dead church, but who love the Lord, that they will be clothed in white and will take part in the Rapture.

Here we see that even in dead churches there can be found those who have been born again and who truly love the Lord. These believers who love Jesus but are in a dead church will not have their name blotted from the book of life but will have their name confessed before God and His angels. If you and I know believers who attend dead churches we should not be critical or condemning, but rather encourage them in the Lord, His Word, and His promises.

LAODICEA: Rev.3:14-22

The next church that comes under the Lord's condemnation is the church of Laodicea. He accuses them of being lukewarm and warns them that He will vomit them out of His mouth. Why such a harsh condemnation? I believe Jesus uses such strong language here because a lukewarm church can do more harm to the work of the Kingdom than a cold church. A lukewarm church can lull believers to sleep, deceiving them that they are being taught the truth of God's Word when in fact they are not.

Naked: not clothed in His righteousness.

Blind: not seeing the truth of the Word.

Poor: being destitute of faith and the riches of His grace.

He encourages them to repent that they might be rich in the things of God. He encourages them to repent because His chastisement is out of love. Verse

20 is one of the most sobering verses in scripture, *"Behold, I stand at the door and knock. If anyone hears My voice and opens the door, I will come in to him and dine with him, and he with Me."* Jesus will never force His way into our hearts; He desires that we should open the door to our hearts eagerly to invite Him in. This is one of the reasons we should never pressure others into believing because if they only "believe" because of our pressure, someone else's pressure could discourage them from believing. For this reason our witness to others should not be from a negative perspective, pointing out all their sins and telling them how awful their life will be, but rather tell them about the love and mercy of God. We also should not give false promises. Jesus never promises health, wealth, or any worldly treasure. Our witness should simply be the promise of the forgiveness of sin, assurance of heaven, and an abundant life in Him that is greater than any worldly gain. Notice, that even to those churches which Jesus has no encouragement for, yet He does encourage the individual believer.

CHAPTER 3

EPHESUS, PERGAMOS, AND THYATIRA
RECEIVE MIXED REVIEWS FROM JESUS

EPHESUS: Rev.2:1-7

Now we come to the three churches which receive
mixed reviews. As we read the Lord's letter it helps us
to understand Paul's epistle to the church at Ephesus.
Here Jesus praises them for their patience and labor
of love. He commends them for not tolerating the evil
teachings of this world, and for not accepting those
who claim they are hearing from the Lord, but test
what is being said against scripture. Also, they were
not afraid to call false teachers liars. They remained
steadfast and did not grow weary in the work of the
Gospel. Very interestingly Jesus also encourages them
in their disdain for the deeds of the Nicolaitans. The
Nicolaitans were those churches that have the clergy
ruling over the lay-people of the church. So apparently
the Church of Ephesus took a stand against this
practice which had already become prevalent. There

are churches today that teach the pastor holds the so-called "umbrella of salvation" over the members of his church; this is the teaching of the Nicolaitans. The deeds of the Nicolaitans would also include those churches that have an ecclesiastical and governmental hierarchy. The pastor's call is to preach and teach the Word of God, period. It is the Holy Spirit alone who holds people accountable and convicts them of sin. Men can never do the work of the Holy Spirit, but should allow Him to work the Word of God into the soul and spirit.

With all this praise from the Lord He still has some criticism for them, He tells the Ephesians they have left their first love. What the Lord means by this is that in our service *to* the Lord we must not forget that our first love must remain the Lord *Himself.* Our aim, our goal, our purpose in all our *service* is fellowship and communion with Him. Communion and fellowship with He himself, not works of service, must always be our highest goal and purpose. Jesus even goes so far as to say that if they don't repent of their confused priorities, He will remove their lampstand; in other words, the church will die. Not every building with a congregation doing churchy activities and even good works of service is a church in the eyes of God. Every church and every believer must examine themselves and ask of Jesus, 'Lord, have I left my first love?' I believe we may find that it is much easier to slide into apostacy when we are too busy then it is to slide into apostasy when we are feeling dry and dull. In any case, Jesus makes it clear that repentance is the only way to be restored to a loving worshiping church. As long as we have breath in our lungs, the Lord gives us opportunity to repent. Praise the Lord! His mercy endures forever!

PERGAMOS: Rev. 2:2-17

Jesus references that Pergamos is located where Satan had his stronghold and yet they held fast to the Name of Jesus, and had not denied the faith. '*The faith*' can be defined simply as salvation by grace through faith alone (Eph.2:8,9). Also consider that Jude exhorted believers to "*contend for the faith that was once for all delivered to the saints*" (Jude 3). A well-known Christian by the name of Antipas was martyred in Pergamos and yet that did not deter the faith or work for the Lord of the believers in this church. Yet this faithful church had a few problems, they held to the doctrine of Balaam who had put a stumbling block in the path of Israel (Numbers 25:1; 2 Pet.2:15; Jude 11), and there were those in the Pergamos church who were doing the very same thing. The 'doctrine of Balaam' was to embolden believers to eat things sacrificed to idols and to commit sexual immorality. We find these prohibitions were among those which the first church counsel determined were to be strictly adhered to (Acts15:29). We might say that doesn't apply today, but of course it does. I'm not sure about 'things sacrificed to idols' however, fornication is deemed totally acceptable among many in today's church. Because this sin simply isn't addressed we now see that homosexuality is tolerated to the peril of souls. If these trends remain unchecked what will be next? Jesus hasn't changed His mind and sin is still sin. Jesus also warns the church that they approved the doctrine of the Nicolaitans which He hates. Take note that Jesus not only disapproves of but hates clerical hierarchy. A true pastor is a servant who has been called to lead by example and to teach and preach the word of God. The only one we are to be submissive to spiritually is our Lord Jesus Christ.

THYATIRA: Rev. 2:18-19

It is interesting that Jesus has more to say to the church of Thyatira than He does to any of the others. They were hard workers in love, service, and faith, in fact Jesus says their good works had grown. Yet, the Lord has this against them, that they allowed 'that woman Jezebel' to be regarded and respected as a prophetess while at the same time she is encouraging the children of God to be involved in sexual immorality and to eat foods which had been sacrificed to idols, which is the same offense as the doctrine of Balaam. The Lord gave this woman time to repent of her sexual immorality and she refused. Notice that Jesus is not addressing the whole church at this point but only the woman. However, the church also receives condemnation for allowing her to have influence in the church. Jesus warns that she will be cast into a sickbed. Tribulation is also guaranteed to come their way unless they repent, and those who follow this doctrine, i.e. "all her children," will suffer the second death. This should be a lesson to all believers that Jesus not only knows but judges our hearts and even our thoughts. To those who did not fall to her false doctrine, which Jesus calls the depths of Satan, He will put no other burden on them but to hold fast to their faith until He comes for His church.

As we look at these churches it is important for us as individual Christians to consider what these letters are saying to us personally, whether good or bad, as well as how it might apply to our local church. Our Lord's warnings are never without hope, but an encouragement to repent. Our condition spiritually is not set in stone but can be changed by simply repenting, *"If we confess our sins, He is faithful and just to forgive us our sins and to cleanse us from all unrighteousness,"* (1 John 1:9). I don't think there can be anything more encouraging than this verse. What we are does not have to be who we shall be. Hope is the greatest encourage-ment to any believer who desires to grow in the Lord. Remember these seven letters where written to churches past, present, and future. Therefore, they are worth reading over with this attitude, '*what is the Lord saying to me?*'

Before we conclude our study on the churches, we must make a careful observation of the conclusion of each letter. These conclusions are only encouraging to those who have eyes to see and ears to hear. Don't cover your eyes and ears to what the Lord might be trying to show you. I would encourage you to make a careful study of the conclusion of each letter:

1. To Ephesus: "*To him who overcomes I will give to eat from the tree of life, which is in the midst of the Paradise of God,*" (Revelation 2:7).
2. To Smyrna: "*He who overcomes shall not be hurt by the second death,*" (Revelation 2:11).
3. To Pergamos: "*To him who overcomes I will give some of the hidden manna to eat. And I will give him a white stone, and on the stone a new name written which no one knows except him who receives it,*" (Revelation 2:17).
4. To Philadelphia: "*He who overcomes, I will make him a pillar in the temple of My God, and he shall go out no more. I will write on him the name of My God and the name of the city of My God, the New Jerusalem, which comes down out of heaven from My God. And I will write on him My new name,*" (Revelation 3:12-13).

5. To Laodicea: *"To him who overcomes I will grant to sit with Me on My throne, as I also overcame and sat down with My Father on His throne,"* (Revelation 3:21).
6. To every church: *"He who has an ear, let him hear."* This has two implications to it: first, God is speaking to us and second, we must be willing to listen.

Notice there are no overcoming promises given to the churches of Sardis and Laodicea as they had fully forsaken the Lord but, we must remember He *did* give promises to individuals in these churches who held to their faith and where willing to repent. We must always remember that any of these warnings that apply to us are not necessarily our permanent condition but may be altered by simply confessing and repenting of our sin and returning to our first love.

CHAPTER 4

VISION OF GOD'S THRONE

In chapter 4 of Revelation, John is taken up to behold the beautiful throne in heaven. The description of this throne is almost as majestic as that of the description of the resurrected, glorified Christ.

Vs.1-3: *"After these things I looked, and behold, a door standing open in heaven. And the first voice which I heard was like a trumpet speaking with me, saying, "Come up here, and I will show you things which must take place after this." Immediately I was in the Spirit; and behold, a throne set in heaven, and One sat on the throne. And He who sat there was like a jasper and a sardius stone in appearance; and there was a rainbow around the throne, in appearance like an emerald."*

This 'door standing open in heaven' is not the rapture as some mistakenly teach. Simple logic is that John was taken up and given this experience nearly 2,000 years ago, and the rapture did not take place at that time. Simple logic tells us, if this is speaking of the rapture, then the martyred souls would not still be under the altar in Chapter Six. Also, the church will <u>first</u> *meet the Lord in the air* (1 Thess.4:17), and <u>then</u> be taken to heaven. Looking at the context, we read here that John is "in the spirit," he is not bodily taken to heaven as Enoch and Elijah were. In addition, in 2 Cor. 12:2 Paul gives the account where he also was taken to the third heaven. Here, in Chapter Four and verse one Jesus tells John, *"I will show you things which must take place after this,"* and so we understand that John is called to heaven "in the spirit" for the express purpose of <u>giving to him the revelation of things to come</u>. The first thing John sees is God's throne, and its description if magnificent.

This all happened while John was 'in the spirit' and while we cannot state exactly what John experienced in these instances, I believe that this was not a bodily experience <u>although it was absolutely real</u> (2Cor.4:18; Heb.11:1). Three other times in the Revelation we read that John was *in the spirit* (1:10; 17:3; and 21:10). Whatever his experience was it is not to be mistaken with the "out of body" experiences claimed by spiritualists. One must be born of the Spirit (John 3:3-7) before one can be "in the spirit". It is only in the spirit that we are capable of discerning the things of God. Please read 1 Cor.2:10-16; Romans 8:14; Gal.5:16, & 25 and John 4:24.

Our attention is then immediately brought to the One seated on the throne, One whose appearance can only be described with inadequate human terms. It is worth noting that the two stones used to describe His appearance, jasper and sardius, have significant meaning. Jasper was the last stone in the breastplate of the high priest and first in the foundation of the New Jerusalem. Sardius is the first stone in the breastplate of the high priest and the sixth stone of the New Jerusalem. The stones in the breastplate of the high priest represented the twelve tribes of Israel. There was a rainbow around the throne, interestingly green like an emerald. The rainbow represents God's promise to man: all who call upon His Name will be saved and not perish. This promise is greater than the first appearance of the rainbow which only promised that God would never again judge the world with water. However the promise represented by the rainbow here is the promise of eternal life, *"For, 'whoever calls on the name of the Lord shall be saved,'"* (Romans 10:13 and Heb.6:12). Therefore all men are without excuse if they fail to call upon the Lord and receive His free gift of salvation.

Vs.4-5: *"Around the throne were twenty four thrones, and on the thrones I saw twenty four elders sitting, clothed in white robes; and they had crowns of gold on their heads. And from the throne proceeded lightnings, thunderings, and voices. Seven lamps of fire were burning before the throne, which are the seven Spirits of God."*

Some believe that the twenty-four elders consist of the twelve patriarchs plus the twelve apostles. However I don't believe this to be the case for the simple reason that John is witnessing this scene while being one of the twelve apostles and is still alive at the time of this experience. I believe in all likelihood the 24 elders are a special creation of celestial beings.

In the description of the throne, we see seven lamps of fire that burn before it. These are the seven Spirits of God. The number seven means complete, the complete power and work of the Holy Spirit is to fill our lamps not partially but completely. Either our "light" is our own fleshly effort, or the power of the Holy Spirit. Jesus said, *"If ... the light that is in you is darkness how great is that darkness,"* (Matt.6:23). Sometimes we can attempt to create our own spiritual light when the only true light comes from the Lord. He alone can fill us with His Spirit of love, *"You are all children of the light and children of the day. We do not belong to the night or to the darkness"* (1 Thess.5:5 see also John 8:12). *"For with You is the fountain of life; in your light we see light,"* (Psalm. 36:9).

Vs.6-8: *"Before the throne there was a sea of glass, like crystal. And in the midst of the throne, and around the throne, were four living creatures full of eyes in front and in back. The first living creature was like a lion, the second living creature like a calf, the third living creature had a face like a man, and the fourth living creature was like a flying eagle. The four living creatures, each having six wings, were full of eyes around and within. And they do not rest day or night, saying: "Holy, holy, holy, lord God Almighty, who was and is and is to come!"*

The sea of glass represents perfect peace and tranquility. In His presence we find perfect peace and tranquility, outside of His presence we find anxious, striving man. Isaiah 26:3 informs us, *"You will keep him in perfect peace, whose mind is stayed on You, because he trusts in You."* Perhaps these four living creatures are the same ones which Ezekiel saw in his vision (Ezek.4:1-10), but in any case, the most important matter for us is to, by faith, try to grasp the majesty and glory of God, and the unhindered worship and adoration which is due Him. *"And they do not rest day or night, saying: 'Holy, holy, holy, lord God Almighty, who was and is and is to come.'"* (Rev.4:8)

Vs.9-11: *"Whenever the living creatures give glory and honor and thanks to Him who sits on the throne, who lives forever and ever, the twenty-four elders fall down before Him who sits on the throne and worship Him who lives forever and ever, and cast their crowns before the throne, saying: "You are worthy, O Lord, To receive glory and honor and power; For You created all things, And by Your will they exist and were created."*

God is not only worthy, but He is also the only one to receive our praise, honor, and glory, for He alone is God. After this powerful description of the throne of God we then move on to the activity John saw taking place in this heavenly scene.

CHAPTER 5

THE SLAIN LAMB OF GOD IS WORTHY
TO TAKE THE SCROLL

vs.1-7: *"And I saw in the right hand of Him who sat on the throne a scroll written inside and on the back, sealed with seven seals. Then I saw a strong angel proclaiming with a loud voice, "Who is worthy to open the scroll and to loose its seals?" And no one in heaven or on the earth or under the earth was able to open the scroll, or to look at it. So I wept much, because no one was found worthy to open and read the scroll, or to look at it. But one of the elders said to me, "Do not weep. Behold, the Lion of the tribe of Judah, the Root of David, has prevailed to open the scroll and to loose its seven seals." And I looked, and behold, in the midst of the throne and of the four living creatures, and in the midst of the elders, stood a Lamb as though it had been slain, having seven horns and seven eyes, which are the seven Spirits of God sent out into all the earth.*

Then He came and took the scroll out of the right hand of Him who sat on the throne."

The question is 'what is the significance of the scroll, and why does John weep when there seemed to be no one to open it?' I believe the scroll could only be the title deed to Planet Earth. In ancient times when a title deed was filed two copies were made. One copy was open so that all parties, or anyone, could examine the contents, and the other copy was sealed to insure that the deed had not been tampered with. Seven seals would indicate the most secure document. Here it is extremely important to understand that the **seals themselves did not constitute the content of the scroll** but simply secured the validity and integrity of the scroll. The person who had the authority and legal right to open the scroll must first open its seals. For this reason the seals had to be clearly authenticated by the one opening the scroll in order to give full assurance that its contents were legitimate. **This why the seals are only meant to be proof that what is contained in the scroll is from its originator**—in this case, the originator of the title deed to Planet Earth is the Lord God Creator of Heaven and Earth. *"Indeed heaven and the highest heavens belong to the Lord your God, also the earth with all that is in it,"* (Deut. 10:14-15). *"The heavens are Yours, the earth also is Yours; The world and all its fullness, You have founded them. The north and the south, You have created them,"*(Ps 89:11-12).

"*The earth is the Lord's, and all its fullness, the world and those who dwell therein. For He has founded it upon the seas, and established it upon the waters,*" (Ps 24:1-2).

All authority in heaven and earth are the Lord's (Matt.28:18). However, God entrusted the first man, Adam with dominion over the earth. Tragically, Adam forfeited dominion to Satan when he chose to heed the word of Satan and doubt the word of God. Satan's powerful enticement to doubt was presented by a simple question, "*Has God indeed said...*" (Gen.3:1emphasis added; see also Matt.6:24). Romans 6:16 informs us, "*Don't you know that when you offer yourselves to someone to obey him as slaves, you are slaves to the one whom you obey...[NIV].*"

Ever since, Satan has been the prince of this world, and if the title deed is not redeemed then the earth would stay permanently under the dominion of Satan. John understood this and that is why he cried. John wept at the thought of Satan remaining in control of earth but then one of the elders informs him that the Lion of the tribe of Judah has prevailed.

Vs.8-14: "*Now when He had taken the scroll, the four living creatures and the twenty-four elders fell down before the Lamb, each having a harp, and golden bowls full of incense, which are the prayers of the saints. And they sang a new song, saying:*" *You are worthy to take the scroll, and to open its seals;*

For You were slain, and have redeemed us to God by Your blood out of every tribe and tongue and people and nation, and have made us kings and priests to our God; And we shall reign on the earth." Then I looked, and I heard the voice of many angels around the throne, the living creatures, and the elders; and the number of them was ten thousand times ten thousand, and thousands of thousands, saying with a loud voice: "Worthy is the Lamb who was slain to receive power and riches and wisdom, and strength and honor and glory and blessing!" And every creature which is in heaven and on the earth and under the earth and such as are in the sea, and all that are in them, I heard saying: "Blessing and honor and glory and power be to Him who sits on the throne, and to the Lamb, forever and ever!" Then the four living creatures said, "Amen!" And the twenty-four elders fell down and worshiped Him who lives forever and ever."

The King James and New King James are the only two translations that render this verse, "redeemed *us*"; all others read, "redeemed **_men_**," or "*them*" NIV, "and with your blood you *purchased men* for God." The mistaken translation of "us" has fueled the erroneous view that the rapture of the church has already taken place, when in fact the rapture, we will find, is further on in John's record. As stated earlier I believe that the twenty-four elders and the living creatures are heavenly beings distinct from angels but who also have no need of redemption.

We understand that the seals are not the content of the scroll but are rather the evidence or guarantee that the contents of the scroll had not been tampered with or altered, and that the actual scroll itself contains the final chapter of earth's history, the Tribulation. Contrary to traditional teaching which has contributed to much of the confusion and difficulty people have in understanding the chronological flow of the book of Revelation, the seals do not begin the unveiling of God's judgment upon planet earth but are there to verify that the final chapter of earth's history as recorded by John is both true and authoritative. John weeps because no one was worthy to open the scroll and reveal the final chapter of planet earth. John then sees the Lamb of God and describes His flawless credentials as the perfect sacrifice for all man's sins and who alone is worthy to open the scroll. The first man Adam forfeited his dominion over planet earth which had been given to him by God and so God became man (John 1:1; Col.2:9; Heb. 1:1-4) in order to redeem man and to destroy the works of the devil (1John 3:8). *"For there is one God and one Mediator between God and men, the Man Christ Jesus, who gave Himself a ransom for all, to be testified in due time,"* (1 Tim 2:5-7). For this reason one of Jesus' many titles is the "last Adam" (1Cor.15:45). The Lamb then takes the scroll from the right hand of God to open it and view its contents.

In this chapter we also have described for us what a worship service in heaven looks like. This is a beautiful testimony of the worthiness of Jesus Christ not only to open the scroll, but of His position as Lord and King of the Universe. Only the Lord of heaven and earth is worthy to reveal the final chapter of man's history, and only He has known from the very beginning what the end would be, proclaiming what shall be as if it has already happened (see Isaiah 42:9 and 46:8-10). We see another example of Jesus proclaiming what shall be as if it had already happened in John 13:31-32 where Jesus speaks in the present tense and yet He had not yet gone to the cross, but in God's economy it was already accomplished, because He knows and sees His will as done. *"So, when he had gone out, Jesus said, 'Now the Son of Man is glorified, and God is glorified in Him. If God is glorified in Him, God will also glorify Him in Himself, and glorify Him immediately."*

As we discussed earlier, it is mistakenly taught in many circles that the seals are an overview of the entire Tribulation period which is the wrath of God. However as we stated earlier the seals are not the content of the scroll but are affixed to the outside. The final seven years of man's history during which God's righteous judgment will be administered to planet earth cannot commence until Jesus has taken His Bride, the Church, to Himself. This will be covered in greater detail a little further on.

Also in vs.11-12, we find another commonly taught error that the "*great multitude*" mentioned here is the church. **However the clear reading of this portion identifies this great multitude as angels, the living creatures, and the elders.** "*Then I looked, and I heard the voice of many <u>angels</u> around the throne, the <u>living creatures</u>, and <u>the elders</u>; and the number of them was ten thousand times ten thousand, and thousands of thousands, saying with a loud voice: 'Worthy is the Lamb who was slain To receive power and riches and wisdom, And strength and honor and glory and blessing!*"(emphasis added).

It is very important to see the simple chronology:

- John is on the island worshiping.
- John is in the spirit where he is shown the glorified Jesus.
- John is shown the scroll.
- John then sees Jesus take the scroll by virtue of His redeeming sacrifice on the cross.
- Jesus then prepares to open the seals which have been affixed to the outside of the scroll for security reasons.

CHAPTER 6

SEALS 1-4: THE FOUR HORSEMEN OF MAN'S HISTORY; THE FIFTH SEAL: THE SOULS UNDER THE ALTAR AND THE RAPTURE OF THE CHURCH THE SIXTH SEAL: COSMIC DISTURBANCES/ EZEKIEL CHAPTER 38

Once again, it cannot be emphasized often enough or strongly enough that the seals are not the content of the scroll. The seals are there to assure the reader that what is contained in the scroll is authoritative and trustworthy. We can clearly understand that the first four seals are authentic because they describe events which are common to man's history. These events have been happening continuously on earth since the fall of man, and are not confined to a particular segment of time. In other words the conditions described in the first four seals are NOT occurring sequentially but rather describe events and conditions which continue to unfold up to the present day and which have clearly reoccurred over and over throughout mankind's history. As we examine the events, situations, and conditions described in each of the first four seals what we discover is a vivid overview of the shocking history of mankind, and see what it has looked like to have Satan rule the world. However, I believe the conditions described will continue to ramp up and become more and more fierce and vicious in their scope and effect upon the entire world stage as time goes on. The heart of man has "waxed cold" (Matt.24:12) and he has become exceedingly proficient in the means by which atrocities can be committed on both small and large scales. Furthermore, it is paramount to observe that the first four seals describe situations which men have themselves effected upon the world; they do not describe situations or conditions which God has affected. In other words, only the first four seals describe conditions which originated with man and have a resulting horizontal effect. The seals are heaven's record of mankind's history. Notice, on the other hand, that almost every condition and situation described, once the Trumpets begin to sound, are effects which have their origin in Heaven <u>and are supernatural occurrences</u>. Because of the common nature of the conditions described in the first four seals, we know beyond a shadow of a doubt that the first four seals are not the commencement of the Tribulation. Regarding the Tribulation period Jesus made the distinctly clarifying stipulation when He said, *"For then there will be great tribulation, <u>such as has not been since the beginning of the world until this time, no, nor ever shall be</u>"* (Matt.24:21 emphasis added). As horrific as mankind's history has been as described in the first four seals, still it's very familiar information. On the other hand, the world has not yet ever seen anything like that which the Tribulation will bring! Think about it, the Tribulation is God judging an unbelieving, unrepenting, Christ rejecting world for all of the things laid out in the first four seals. The fifth, sixth, and seventh seals are altogether different in their scope and purpose from the first four. The fifth, sixth, and seventh seals do not describe conditions in the world as it has always been throughout human history but are entirely supernatural occurrences. We will cover them in greater detail when we come to those seals. I believe there is the strongest evidence that the Rapture of the Church occurs when the fifth seal is opened and the martyred souls receive their white robe. I do not believe the martyred souls receive a white robe apart from the rest of the church. The sixth seal is God's faithful intervention in the war of Ezekiel 38 when He rescues the nation Israel, and is the prelude to the Tribulation which begins with the trumpet judgments.

Vs.1-2: THE FIRST SEAL

"Now I saw when the Lamb opened one of the seals; and I heard one of the four living creatures saying with a voice like thunder, 'Come and see.' And I looked, and behold, a white horse. He who sat on it had a bow; and a crown was given to him, and he went out conquering and to conquer."

I believe that the personage riding the white horse is allegorical to Satan. The world has been in upheaval since the fall, with wars, murder, and every inhumanity man can perpetrate upon his fellow man. Satan is doing all he can to destroy God's perfect creation and to conquer the world for evil. When Satan deceived Eve, and she and Adam chose to disobey God, that choice resulted in Adam forfeiting dominion to Satan (Gen.1:27-31). Henceforth, Satan has been the prince of this world (John 12:31; 14:30; 16:11; Ephesians 2:2-3) and I believe that's when he was given a crown. Since that incident in the Garden Satan continues to deceive man by his control over planet earth, and his intent has been to destroy man, God's special creation. *"The thief does not come except to steal, and to kill, and to destroy,"* (John 10:10). This is the world's history: war and conquest along with the resulting death and suffering.

This rider has a crown by virtue of deception but he is not the king, and we who are saved are no longer subject to this evil prince but are now ruled by our glorious King Jesus Christ. God has *"delivered us from the power of darkness and conveyed us into the kingdom of the Son of His love". . . that you may proclaim the praises of Him who called you out of darkness into His marvelous light,"* (Col. 1:13 & 1 Pet.2:9). But, while in the flesh we are still subject to the effects of a fallen world. The drive for conquest and the resulting wars and disputes which Satan inspires will reach a crescendo in the fulfillment of Ezekiel 38.

I do not believe that the riders are actual historical persons and are therefore not confined to any one period of history, but are an allegorical portrayal of the particular devastation each of them brings. Rather than being limited to any particular period of time, each has been "riding" ever since Satan stole dominion over Planet Earth from Adam. Without a doubt, the riders symbolize the demonic influences that have certainly been at work throughout the history of the world. We must realize that the events described are not initiated with the opening of that particular seal but merely disclose heaven's record. The remaining three horsemen continue the disclosure of that dark record.

Vs.3-4: THE SECOND SEAL

The second seal refers to conflict on earth; not only war, but internal, regional, and national upheaval on earth, *"When He opened the second seal, I heard the second living creature saying, 'Come and see.' Another horse, fiery red, went out. And it was granted to the one who sat on it to take peace from the earth, and that people should kill one another; and there was given to him a great sword."*

Since Adam and Eve were cast out of the Garden there has been a lot of killing beginning with their own son taking the life of his brother. Killing is at an all time high in the world, not only in wars and gang violence, but in the killing of the most innocent. According to *The London Telegraph* on March 24, 2014, aborted and miscarried babies are used to heat offices. On Jan 18, 2012, an Oklahoma bill was introduced to ban the sale of food containing aborted fetuses. Cosmetics, vaccines, and even food research uses fetuses. Gang violence, random killing, drug-related deaths, and suicide are pandemic in the world, paled only by the sacrifice of the unborn upon the altar of convenience. By rejecting the Creator and instead believing the lie that man is a random product of evolution, the sanctity of life has been lost. With all of the vehement rhetoric about human rights it is apparent that very few have any regard for human life. The rider on the red horse has certainly had a great measure of victory on planet earth.

Once again notice this is not the tribulation, which is God's judgment upon the world, but the history of man since the fall. Man, in his selfishness and greed, killing and robbing one another for personal gain, is without a doubt under the influence and sway of the Prince of this world. *"Where do wars and fights come from among you? Do they not come from your desires for pleasure that war in your members? You lust and do not have. You murder and covet and cannot obtain. You fight and war ....Do you not know that friendship with the world is enmity with God? Whoever therefore wants to be a friend of the world makes himself an enemy of God." "Do not love the world or the things in the world. If anyone love the world, the love of the Father is not in him. For all that is in the world – the lust of the flesh, the lust of the eyes, and the pride of life – is not of the Father but is of the world. And the world is passing away, and the lust of it." However dear brothers and sisters, "We know that we are of God, and the whole world lies under the sway of the wicked one,"* (James 4:1-4; 1 John 2:15-17 & 5:19).

God created the world to be at peace with Him, and mankind with one another. Sadly, since the fall, man has sought for peace and purpose in every way except to simply come back to his loving Creator God. We will discover that man, along with the governments and systems which man has organized, will only have peace when the Prince of Peace comes and reigns on earth from the throne of David. But until that time, we are commissioned to spread the truth of His salvation which is the only way to escape Satan's grip. Believers are described as, *"a peculiar people"* (1 Pet.2:9 KJV). In other words, by virtue of being filled with and led by the Holy Spirit, believers are strangely different than those ruled by the flesh and Satan, and his world system.

Since the fall of man, atonement for sin required the shedding of innocent blood. Yahweh Himself provided the first offering to cover Adam and Eve (Gen.3:21), and later He required blood as the only prescription for sin. *"For the life of the flesh is in the blood, and I have given it to you upon the altar to make atonement for your souls; for it is the blood that makes atonement for the soul,"* (Lev.17:11-12). *"...And without the shedding of blood there is no remission,"* (Heb. 9:22). Furthermore, we are instructed throughout the book of Hebrews that the Law was merely a shadow of things to come and not the true thing itself (Heb.10:1-4), and that, *"it is not possible that the blood of bulls and goats could take away sins"* (vs.4). For this reason God sent His only begotten Son into the world. Jesus had to clothe Himself in flesh and become one of us in order to permanently atone for the sin of mankind. *"...Who, being in the form of God, did not consider it robbery to be equal with God, but made Himself of no reputation, taking the form of a bondservant, and coming in the likeness of men. And being found in appearance as a man, He humbled Himself and became obedient to the point of death, even the death of the cross,"* (Phil

2:6-8). *"And the Word became flesh and dwelt among us, and we beheld His glory, the glory as of the only begotten of the Father, full of grace and truth"* . . . *For the law was given through Moses, but grace and truth came through Jesus Christ. No one has seen God at any time. The only begotten Son, who is in the bosom of the Father, He has declared Him"* (John 1:14 & 17-18 read also Heb. 10:5-10). Here is a small sampling of what the Blood of the Lamb has accomplished for sinners:

> Acts 20:28 - Purchases souls
> Romans 3:25 - Makes propitiation
> Romans 5:9 - Justifies
> Ephesians 1:7 & Rev.5:9 - Brings redemption & forgiveness
> Ephesians 2:13- Brings us near
> Colossians 1:20 - Brings peace
> Hebrews 10:19 - Gains us entrance to the Holiest of Holies!!!
> Matt.1:21 & Rev. 1:5 7:14 - Washes/frees us from sin
> Rev. 12:11- Power to overcome Satan
> Hebrews 13:12 - Sanctifies

I have been redeemed by the blood of the Lamb and my redemption is secure in Him, but I look forward to the day when my redemption is complete, when

I turn in this mortal body for a new glorified body. *"The last enemy that will be destroyed is death,"* (1 Corinthians 15:26). *"So also is the resurrection of the dead. The body is sown in corruption, it is raised in incorruption. It is sown in dishonor, it is raised in glory. It is sown in weakness, it is raised in power. It is sown a natural body, it is raised a spiritual body. There is a natural body, and there is a spiritual body,"* (1 Corinthians 15:42-44).

Vs.5-6: THE THIRD SEAL

"When He opened the third seal, I heard the third living creature say, 'Come and see.' So I looked, and behold, a black horse, and he who sat on it had a pair of scales in his hand. And I heard a voice in the midst of the four living creatures saying, 'A quart of wheat for a denarius, and three quarts of barley for a denarius; and do not harm the oil and the wine.'

The opening of the third seal reveals the record of inflation, famine, and a scarcity of food on earth, conditions which have always been present. Not many people are aware of the fact that if something were to disrupt transport nationwide, store shelves in the United States are only three days from being empty. Most of us do not possess the skill and resourcefulness of past generations who knew how to keep chickens, milk cows, tend gardens, and do canning. For the most part, most of us are fully dependent upon commercial food. An economic collapse could very well result in all the four horsemen reaching their apex in concert together. Ask yourself this question: 'what will people do for food when they are hungry?' The answer is, they will do anything to survive.

There have been many explanations given concerning the last statement of this seal, *"do not harm the oil and the wine."* I have read many but none have answered the question for me. I believe there is a strong clue in that it is a *"voice from heaven"* which issues the restriction, *'do not harm the oil and the wine.'* It very well could refer to the fact that spiritual nourishment is always plentiful and free to those who seek the truth. God's blessings and favor are not subject to world conditions, and His love and mercy have never been withheld from the repentant soul. Listen to our loving God's voice pleading through His servant Isaiah, *"Ho! Everyone who thirsts, come to the waters; and you who have no money, come, buy and eat. Yes, come, buy wine and milk without money and without price. Why do you spend money for what is not bread, and your wages for what does not satisfy? Listen carefully to Me, and eat what is good, and let your soul delight itself in abundance,"* (Isaiah 55:1-2).

Vs.7-8: THE FOURTH SEAL

*"When He opened the fourth seal, I heard the voice
of the fourth living creature saying, 'Come and see.'
So I looked, and behold, a pale horse. And the name of
him who sat on it was Death, and Hades followed with
him. And power was given to them over a fourth of the
earth, to kill with sword, with hunger, with death, and
by the beasts of the earth."*

The fourth Seal refers to widespread death on
Earth. Again, the horror of genocide and famine are
nothing new to planet earth. The rider of the pale
horse depicts the dark agenda of great destruction to
human life. This rider's agenda is death by any means.
Remember that none of the first four seals are confined
to a particular segment of time but together in concert
give us an overview of all of Earth's history up to
the present. We are all too familiar with this rider's
devastating work. Also notice, that Hades followed
with him, I believe to collect those who are not saved.
Obviously, countless numbers of God's redeemed have
died by disease, in accidents, in battle, etc and have
personally experienced that to be absent from the body
is to be present with the Lord (2 Cor. 5:8). But, to die
without Christ is by far the greatest tragedy of all.
Death is the last enemy to be destroyed (1Cor.15:26)
and this rider's work will not end until Jesus returns
to Earth to set up His Kingdom at which time death

and Hades will both be thrown into the lake of fire (Rev.20:12-14).

Vs.9-11: THE FIFTH SEAL

"When He opened the fifth seal, I saw under the altar the souls of those who had been slain for the word of God and for the testimony which they held. And they cried with a loud voice, saying, 'How long, O Lord, holy and true, until You judge and avenge our blood on those who dwell on the earth?' Then a white robe was given to each of them; and it was said to them that they should rest a little while longer, until both the number of their fellow servants and their brethren, who would be killed as they were, was completed."

The martyred souls under the altar are given a place of special honor and comfort in God's presence. These are not the Tribulation martyrs as is often erroneously taught, but these are those who have died for their faith throughout history. For example, it is estimated 36 million believers died during the Roman Inquisition alone! According to Open Doors USA in its recently published "World Watch List 2019" it was stated that, "4,136 Christians were killed for faith-related reasons. On average, that's 11 Christians killed every day for their faith. Additionally, "2,625 Christians were detained without trial, arrested, sentenced and imprisoned," in 2018 and, "1,266 churches or Christian buildings were attacked".

These precious martyred souls are not asking, "how long until the rapture and you get us out from under here" nor are they asking about Christ's return to earth. They ask, <u>how long until their blood is avenged for</u>! This is not a request for revenge on any one group, or those who were personally responsible for their deaths. On the contrary, they ask in concert regarding the timing of God's judgment on an unbelieving earth that has persecuted believers since the beginning, from the blood of righteous Able, to the last martyred believer. Their blood will be avenged. So we understand that they are not being told to wait under the altar until their blood is avenged, they are simply told to rest until the number of those who will be martyred is complete. Many, many more are about to die for their faith in Jesus Christ. Many will come to salvation during the tribulation, and many will be beheaded for their faith. NOTICE: As soon as they ask the question, <u>and before they are given an answer,</u> they are immediately given a white robe which I believe is a metaphor for their bodies being glorified.

This indicates two things: first, obviously, the rapture had not yet occurred because when the martyred souls under the altar receive their white robes all believers will receive theirs as well. That all believers receive the promised white robe at the same time cannot be stated strongly enough. In 1 Thessalonians 4:13-18 we are clearly instructed that when Jesus comes for His Church He is going to <u>bring with Him</u> the souls of those who have died which obviously would include the martyred saints. This is what is meant in vs. 15 & 17 where we read that those who are alive and remain, <u>until the coming of the Lord</u>, will by no mean precede those who have died, *"The dead in Christ will <u>rise first</u>,"* (vs.16). In other words, the bodies of all those who have died as believers will be resurrected and instantaneously "<u>changed</u>" and what has been "corrupt" will "put on incorruption", and what has been mortal will "put on immortality" (1 Cor. 15:52-55), and be reunited with their soul. *"<u>THEN</u> we who are alive and remain shall be caught up **together with them** in the clouds to meet the Lord in the air"* (vs.17 emphasis added). So we understand that once the souls under the altar receive their white robes they no longer remain under the altar but are reuntied with their resurrected, glorified bodies. THIS IS THE RAPTURE.

1 Thess.4:13-18 clearly describe a supernatural event where the souls of the dead in Christ are united with their glorified and resurrected bodies, and believers who are alive are *"caught up together with them in the clouds to meet the Lord in the air."* The English, *"caught up"* in vs.17 has been rendered from

the words, *harpatzo* (Gk) and *rapturo* (Latin) and has come to be known simply as *rapture*.

Vs.12-17: THE SIXTH SEAL: COSMIC DISTURBANCES AND THE WAR OF EZEK.38

The doctrine of the pre-tribulation rapture is that God's people, His church, must be taken out of the world before His wrath falls on planet earth because scripture has informed us that, *"God did not appoint us to wrath, but to obtain salvation through our Lord Jesus Christ, who died for us, that whether we wake or sleep, we should live together with Him"* (1 Thessalonians 5:9-10). It makes no sense that God would include His Church in His judgment upon the unbelieving and the ungodly. Yes, testing will come; yes some or many may fall away, but this is not God's judgment. God's judgment consists entirely of His wrath displayed in supernatural occurrences never before seen. As evil on the earth reaches its apex, the time has arrived for God's wrath to be poured out on the God rejecting world. However, when the tribulation begins it is not the end of man's chance to be saved. As we will examine later on, many will be saved during the tribulation, but most of them will suffer difficult trials, and even execution for their faith.

Vs.12-17: *"I looked when he opened the sixth seal,*

and behold, there was a great earthquake; and the sun became black as sackcloth of hair, and the moon became like blood. And the stars of heaven fell to the earth, as a fig tree drops its late figs when it is shaken by a mighty wind. Then the sky receded as a scroll when it is rolled up, and every mountain and island was moved out of its place. And the kings of the earth, the great men, the rich men, the commanders, the mighty men, every slave and every free man, hid themselves in the caves and in the rocks of the mountains, and said to the mountains and rocks, 'Fall on us and hide us from the face of Him who sits on the throne and from the wrath of the Lamb! For the great day of His wrath has come, and who is able to stand?"

The rapture of believers is immediately followed by catastrophic cosmic events. Many have been taught that this is describing the Battle of Armageddon. However I will show clearly why that is a mistaken idea. Rather, I believe that the catastrophic events of vs. 12-14, the moment the Lamb opens the sixth seal, is assuredly what is described in Ezekiel 38 when God supernaturally intervenes to rescue the nation Israel. Who are these kings, great and rich men calling for the mountains to fall on them, and why are they there in the first place? It would appear that previous to the opening of the sixth seal a great army had already assembled itself against Israel from the north on the mountains of Israel. Even though the specific nations listed in Ezek. 38-39 which come against Israel for plunder are not named here in Rev.6:15 we can be confident that this is one and the same event because of the other details which are outlined. Here in Rev.6 the primary significance is that the people groups identified are attempting to hide from the face of the Lamb who they can see, and whose identity they know. Many have confused the situation described in Revelation 6:12-17 with that which is described in Revelation 16:16 and 19:17-21. However, Rev. 16:16 and 19:17-21 are one and the same event, the Battle of Armageddon, while Rev.6:12-17 is the war of Ezek. 38. We can make a clear distinction between these events by simply looking at the details provided to us:

Revelation 6:12-17	Ezekiel Chapter 38	Revelation 16:16 & 19:17-21
Great earthquake, cosmic disturbances, kings of the earth, commanders, mighty men, et al hide in caves and rocks of the mountains to hide from the Lamb, acknowledging that the day of His wrath had come and that no one can stand against Him. The Lamb sits on a throne not a horse	Great earthquake, cosmic disturbances, all shake at His presence, mountains thrown down, every man's sword is against his fellow soldier. Then they shall know I am the Lord.	No earthquake, no cosmic disturbances. The Beast and the kings of earth have gathered in a valley for the express purpose to make war against the Lord who sits on a horse. This assembly is immediately defeated, judged and cast into the Lake of Fire.

So we can clearly see that there are not even any similarities between the event described in Rev. 6:12-17/Ezek.38 and those of Rev. 16 & 19. In Revelation Chapter 16:14,16 we are simply informed that armies of the earth gather at Armageddon which is a valley, but the <u>actual battle</u> isn't described until 19:17-21. I believe the reason that Rev. 6:12-17 and Ezekiel Chapter 38 are mistakenly identified with Rev. 16:16 & Rev. 19:17-21 is in large part due to the illogical notion that the seals are an overview of the entire book. This requires the reader to know when he/she must either fast forward, or rewind, rendering the entire book awkward and confusing. When Revelation is read with the understanding that it flows chronologically the entire book becomes plain and clear.

We must ask why is this group of kings, commanders, great men, mighty men, rich and poor, slave and free here in the first place? We find in our study of Ezekiel 38 that these have come against Israel for plunder, or in other words for great financial gain. Particularly they seek Israel's wealth of natural gas. It's not just the mighty and the rich who want to be richer and mightier, the poor and the slave want in on this venture as well. This entire world system is driven by gain and advancement. Those who get caught up in that drive and operate according to this world's system, whether rich or poor, powerful or not, yet are all on the same team whether they know it or not.

We must realize that the backers of a one-world government are the men and women of finance. Everything is about power and money which is the fuel that drives the economic, political, and religious powers of the world. To understand this portion we need to know who the kings and mighty men are that come against Israel. We find the answers in Ezekiel 38 and 39. We must keep in mind that "Gog" is not essentially the name of a nation or an individual, but is a title much like "Czar" or "Ahasuerus". For example, "Jethro" is the title for the priest of Midian, Moses' father-in-law (Ex.3:1), but his name is Reuel (Num.10:29). This title of "Gog" is referenced again in Revelation 20:8 which is probably why Ezekiel 38 and Rev. 6:12-17 are mistakenly identified as the Battle of Armageddon.

However, in Ezekiel Chapter 38 the title "Gog" is specified as the prince (*mighty prince* in Heb. possibly the present leader of Russia) of Rosh, Meshech, and Tubal from Magog; the land north of the Caspian and Black sea, which includes all of Russia, Ukraine, and parts of the other surrounding nations. In biblical times, according to an ancient Turkish map, Turkey was made up of four parts: Meshech, Tubal, Gomer, and Togarmah. Persia was what is present day Iran, Afghanistan, Pakistan, and part of Iraq. Ethiopia and Libya would be present day nations from Sudan up through northern Africa. I feel certain that without

Russia's support these armies would never dare to come against Israel on their own.

Jesus is describing this very event when He said, *"And there will be signs in the sun, in the moon, and in the stars; and on the earth distress of nations, with perplexity, the sea and the waves roaring; men's hearts failing them **from fear and the expectation of those things which are coming on the earth**, for the powers of the heavens will be shaken. Then they will see the Son of Man coming in a cloud with power and great glory. Now when these things **begin** to happen, **look up and lift up your heads**, because your redemption draws near,"* (Luke 21:25-28 emphasis added).

CHAPTER 7

144,000 SEALED SERVANTS
RAPTURED CHURCH SEEN IN HEAVEN

Vs.1-8 : *"After these things I saw four angels standing at the four corners of the earth, holding the four winds of the earth, that the wind should not blow on the earth, on the sea, or on any tree. Then I saw another angel ascending from the east, having the seal of the living God. And he cried with a loud voice to the four angels to whom it was granted to harm the earth and the sea, saying, "Do not harm the earth, the sea, or the trees till we have sealed the servants of our God on their foreheads." And I heard the number of those who were sealed. One hundred and forty-four thousand of all the tribes of the children of Israel were sealed:*

> *of the tribe of Judah twelve thousand were sealed;*
> *of the tribe of Reuben twelve thousand were sealed;*

of the tribe of Gad twelve thousand were sealed;

of the tribe of Asher twelve thousand were sealed;

of the tribe of Naphtali twelve thousand were sealed;

of the tribe of Manasseh twelve thousand were sealed;

of the tribe of Simeon twelve thousand were sealed;

of the tribe of Levi twelve thousand were sealed;

of the tribe of Issachar twelve thousand were sealed;

of the tribe of Zebulun twelve thousand were sealed;

of the tribe of Joseph twelve thousand were sealed;

of the tribe of Benjamin twelve thousand were sealed."

The "four corners of the earth" in verse 1 is not inferring that the earth is a cube but is a common phrase which refers to the entire world. The word rendered here "corners" is from the Greek, *gonia,* literally *quarters.* Isa.40:22 informs us that the Lord "sits above the circle of the earth". The winds are the winds of judgment that are held back by the four angels.

Judgment is delayed while the servants of God, 12,000 from every tribe, (note there are no "lost" tribes) are sealed for some unspecified work of ministry to this condemned world. Obviously, these Jewish men got saved sometime after the rapture and they are sealed just before God's judgment is poured out on the earth.

The fifth angel that is mentioned seems to be quite prominent from the other four because he cries out with a loud or great voice, *phone-megale;* what we get the word *megaphone* from, to the other four to delay their work until the 144,000 have been sealed. The sense is that a frightful and fearful judgment is about to occur. It is the fifth angel who actually has the seal of the Living God to seal this very specific number of Jewish males, 12,000 from each tribe. Because John is given this very specific number to record there are those who believe this must by symbolic however I don't believe that is the case. God has numbered the stars, calls them each by name (Ps.147:4-5), has numbered the hairs on our heads (Lk.12:7), and the number of our days (Job 14;5). He can certainly determine this exact number of Jewish men to be sealed. Ps 147:5 informs us, *"Great is our Lord, and mighty in power; His understanding is infinite."*

There are at least two reasons for the sealing of the 144,000 first, presumably sealed for ministry and second, sealed in order to be protected from God's judgment which is coming upon a sinful world. Later on in Revelation 9:4 this seal of protection upon believers is again referenced, and we have no idea if the 144,000 are sealed in the same way. However, it is a sobering thought to consider how our faith would endure even in this present age if we were not also sealed. *"In Him you also trusted, after you heard the word of truth, the gospel of your salvation; in whom also, having believed, you were sealed with the Holy Spirit of promise, who is the guarantee of our inheritance until the redemption of the purchased possession, to the praise of His glory,"* (Eph.1:13,14 see also 4:40 and 2 Cor.1:21-11). Now that the Church has been raptured out of the world the ministry and work of being God's primary witnesses to the world is returned to the Jews and the seventieth week of Daniel can begin.

Take note that the names of the twelve tribes listed here are different than the original list given in Genesis 49:1-28. First of all, we see that Judah now heads the list because Reuben lost his place for having had relations with his father's wife (Genesis 3:22). We also find that the tribes of Dan and Ephraim have been disqualified altogether for having led the northern kingdom of Israel into idolatry, and the tribe of Levi replaces Dan. Levi wasn't initially given an inheritance by God because He himself was to be their portion (Josh.13:14, 33). It is worth noting that Reuben committed adultery and lost his place but he did receive an inheritance, whereas

Dan and Ephraim committed idolatry and lost both their place and inheritance. We are not told what the ministry of the 144,000 is specifically, however in chapter 14 we will learn a little more about them.

Contrary to what some groups teach these 144,000 do not constitute the total number of Jews who will be saved. *"And it shall come to pass in all the land,' Says the Lord, 'That two-thirds in it shall be cut off and die, But one-third shall be left in it: I will bring the one-third through the fire, Will refine them as silver is refined, And test them as gold is tested. They will call on My name, And I will answer them. I will say, 'This is My people'; And each one will say, 'The Lord is my God'"* (Zechariah 13:8-9); *"For I do not desire, brethren, that you should be ignorant of this mystery, lest you should be wise in your own opinion, that blindness in part has happened to Israel until the fullness of the Gentiles has come in. And so all Israel will be saved, as it is written: 'The Deliverer will come out of Zion, And He will turn away ungodliness from Jacob; For this is My covenant with them, When I take away their sins,"* (Romans 11:25-27). One-third of all Jews will survive the tribulation and will come to faith in their Messiah Jesus.

Vs. 9-10: *"After these things I looked, and behold, a great multitude which no one could number, of all nations, tribes, peoples, and tongues, standing before the throne and before the Lamb, clothed with white robes, with palm branches in their hands, and crying out with a loud voice, saying, "Salvation belongs to our God who sits on the throne, and to the Lamb!"*

This *"great multitude which no one could number,"* is specifically identified as being from *"all nations, tribes, peoples, and tongues,"* and who have on white robes. These are people, and we are informed that no one can number this great multitude. In contrast please note that the group which John sees in Chapter 5:11-12, which is often mistakenly identified as the church, can be numbered: ten thousands of ten thousands and thousands and thousands. Also please note that the group referenced in chapter five is identified specifically as angels, the living creatures, and the elders, not men. And so we understand that here in chapter seven and verse 9-10 we have our first glimpse of the Raptured Church before the throne of God. This incalculable multitude is made up of every ethnic and geographical group in the world and have been here since <u>before</u> the sixth seal was opened. Although it seems like a lot has transpired since the sixth seal was opened in actuality there have been just three developments: (1) The Church has been Raptured, (2) The War of Ezekiel 38 took place, and (3) The 144,000 were sealed. Ponder the great reality that all those who have loved the Lord from the time of creation will be in that group which no one can number.

Vs.11-17: *"All the angels stood around the throne*

and the elders and the four living creatures, and fell on their faces before the throne and worshiped God, saying: "Amen! Blessing and glory and wisdom, Thanksgiving and honor and power and might, Be to our God forever and ever. Amen." Then one of the elders answered, saying to me, "Who are these arrayed in white robes, and where did they come from?" And I said to him, "Sir, you know." So he said to me, "These are the ones who come out of the great tribulation, and washed their robes and made them white in the blood of the Lamb. Therefore they are before the throne of God, and serve Him day and night in His temple. And He who sits on the throne will dwell among them. They shall neither hunger anymore nor thirst anymore; the sun shall not strike them, nor any heat; for the Lamb who is in the midst of the throne will shepherd them and lead them to living fountains of waters. And God will wipe away every tear from their eyes."

At first John did not know who these people are who comprise this large multitude. John is then told that they are those who have come out of the great tribulation. Noah and Lot are early examples of God's taking His people "out" before He pours out judgment. It is so important to not go beyond what the scripture plainly says (1 Cor. 4:6). Jesus made it clear to the church of Philadelphia that He was going to deliver them from "that hour." What hour? The hour that John is talking about right now. We need to let Scripture speak for itself.

Keep in mind, everything John is shown is a <u>vision of what was the future for him,</u> and is still yet the future for us. God shows his servant a *vision* of what is *to be* – not of what is, *"things which will take place after this."* That is why he did not know the identity of this group. I am sure John was shocked to find how large the church would become. This great multitude from all over the world and which includes every people group indicates that evangelism efforts throughout history have been very effective. Also, I personally find it fascinating to think that there are those who will be among this vast number who had previously waved palm branches and proclaimed Jesus as King of Kings and Lord of Lords during His earthly ministry (John 12:12-19). However, shortly after completing his record of the Revelation John would also take his place under the altar with the martyred saints.

"White robes" is a metaphor for the glorified body which believers are given (Phil.3:21) but it also denotes being clothed in His righteousness. Believers are informed in Isa. 54:17 that, *"This is the heritage of the servants of the Lord, and their righteousness is from Me, says the Lord"* . . . *"So the Lord God will cause righteousness and praise to spring forth before all the nations"* (Isa. 61:11). God does not ask us to establish our own righteousness. To attempt to do so constitutes

rebellion, which was His issue with the nation Israel that the prophets addressed many, many times.

Many people say, "I don't deserve such a great reward," and of course none of us do; and being profoundly aware of that fact is cause for us to lift up spontaneous praise and thanksgiving, adoration and worship to our loving and forgiving God. In my opinion this is synonymous with waving palm branches today. Christ not only saves us by faith, not of any of our own effort, but He also saves us completely. There is nothing hanging over our head, no stain or blot that still remains; we are perfectly saved (read Hebrews 7:25). God's gift of salvation is free or it wouldn't be a gift. *"For I delivered to you first of all that which I also received: that Christ died for our sins according to the Scriptures, and that He was buried, and that He rose again the third day according to the Scriptures"* (1 Corinthians 15:3-4). *"But God, who is rich in mercy, because of His great love with which He loved us, even when we were dead in trespasses, made us alive together with Christ (by grace you have been saved), and raise us up together, and made us sit together in the heavenly places in Christ Jesus, that in the ages to come He might show the exceeding riches of His grace in His kindness toward us in Christ Jesus, for by grace you have been saved through faith, and that not of yourselves; it is the gift of God, not of works, lest anyone should boast"* . . . *"And if by grace, then it is no longer of works; otherwise grace is no longer grace,"* (Eph.2:4-9 and Romans 11:6).

No wonder His wrath will be poured out on those who refuse His great gift because they are without excuse. This side of eternity we cannot even fathom that kind of fellowship, communion, and worship that is described in vs.11 and which is unhindered by the flesh and self. And God will wipe away every tear from our eyes. This life is full of disappointment, heartache, and pain which makes this promise very appealing. What should go without saying is that this temple is not the earthly temple which was constructed as a replica of the heavenly temple. This temple in Heaven was not cleansed with the blood of bulls and goats, but with the blood of the Lamb who carried it into the heavenly temple Himself (read Hebrews 9:11-15 and 24). God is in this temple and so God's people are in this temple to serve and worship Him there.

The Conquistadors' quest for gold was a futile one because they had assumed the Muisca Indians of Columbia, South America had a lot of gold when in actuality all they had was a lot of salt. They were searching for gold in the wrong place. Similarly, so much eschatology (the study of end-time events) is based on the mistaken premise that the rapture takes place before the seals are opened, and asserts that the seals are the beginning of the Tribulation. However, we plainly see that the events described in the seals are strictly Heaven's record of mankind's dark history. We cannot begin to fathom the measure of the sheer devastation and chaos that will follow the rapture. Worldwide persecution against believers in Jesus Christ on an unprecedented scale will commence when God's wrath begins to be poured out. I realize that many believers around the world are being persecuted now. However, this will be worldwide martyrdom that will be in the numbers of perhaps hundreds of thousands, probably more. Anyone who does not follow the post-rapture order of things and eventually take the required mark will be put to death.

So, at this point the Church has been caught up to meet the Lord in the air, the sixth seal has been opened and the war of Ezekiel 38 has taken place. Also, the 144,000 Jewish males from each of the twelve tribes have been sealed. Then there is a pause in the narrative to make us aware of what is going on in Heaven as the Church arrives at home. Now, the seventh seal is about to be opened.

However, before we leave these great events, particularly the Rapture of the Church, and begin to cover the very sobering events that commence with the opening of the seventh seal, I think it's very important to make sure we have a firm grasp of the doctrine of imminency. What is the doctrine of Imminency? The word imminent is taken from the Latin *imminere*; "overhanging", "ready to fall," the English word means *about to happen.* Therefore, the doctrine of imminency refers to the expectation of the Lord's return for His Church at any moment. The expectation of the Lord's imminent return began the moment He ascended. The parable of the ten virgins is all about the doctrine of imminency. So, we do not want to leave the subject of the rapture of the church of Jesus Christ without discussing the very important *doctrine of imminency.* There are some very important questions that need to be answered concerning what seem to be contradictory portions. Here's one of them: why do some scriptures say watch and be ready, yet other scriptures say that no one can know the day or the hour when the rapture is to occur? If every generation looked for His imminent return, how can we be so certain that *this is the time?* Let's look at a few verses which state that no one knows exactly when He will return.

1. *"Watch therefore, for you do not know what hour your Lord is coming,"* (Matthew 24:42).
2. *"Afterward the other virgins came also, saying, 'Lord, Lord, open to us!' But he answered and said, 'Assuredly, I say to you, I do not know you.' Watch therefore, for you know neither the day* (hay-mer-ah, twenty-four hour period) *nor the hour* (ho-raw, sixty minutes) *in which the Son of Man is coming,"* (Matthew 25:11-13).

3. *"But of that day and hour no one knows, not even the angels in heaven, nor the Son, but only The Father. Take heed, watch and pray; for you do not know when the time is. It is like a man going to a far country, who left his house and gave authority to his servants, and to each his work, and commanded the doorkeeper to watch. Watch therefore, for you do not know when the master of the house is coming—in the evening, at midnight, at the crowing of the rooster, or in the morning, lest, coming suddenly, he find you sleeping. And what I say to you, I say to all: Watch,"* (Mark 13:32-37).

What is the oxymoron you notice? These verses tell us that we do not know when, but they all say we should be watching. The heart of these verses is that the believer should always be watching and ready for His return, period. In Luke 2:25 and 36-38 we are introduced to two precious believers, Simeon and Anna who are to us wonderful examples of watching. They knew from the scriptures that the timing for Messiah was near and so they were watching every day, and we should be doing the same. So, let's look at some of those verses that say we should not be surprised when He returns for His Church.

1. *"But concerning the times and the seasons, brethren, you have no need that I should write to you. For you yourselves know perfectly that the day of the Lord so comes as a thief in the night. For when they say, "Peace and safety!" then sudden destruction comes upon them, as labor pains upon a pregnant woman. And they shall not escape. But you, brethren, are not in darkness, so that this Day should overtake you as a thief. You are all sons of light and sons of the day. We are not of the night nor of darkness. Therefore let us not sleep, as others do, but let us watch and be sober"* (1 Thessalonians 5:1-6).

2. *"Then the Pharisees and Sadducees came, and testing Him asked that He would show them a sign from heaven. He answered and said to them, "When it is evening you say, 'It will be fair weather, for the sky is red'; and in the morning, 'It will be foul weather today, for the sky is red and threatening.' Hypocrites! You know how to discern the face of the sky, but you cannot discern the signs of the times,"* (Matthew 16:1-3).

Only those who tremble at His Word and study will understand the incredible eternal significance of the times we live in. Again we may ask, if every generation looked for His imminent return, then how can we say this is the time? This question can be answered with one word: Israel. We need to familiarize ourselves with Daniel 9:2; Ezekiel 37:16-17 & 21 because in our day we tend to take for granted the existence of Israel as a nation. But the Nation of Israel is the single greatest miracle of our life time, which could be the subject of another book entirely. A number of O.T. prophets used the fig tree as a metaphor for Israel. For example Joel 1:6-7, 1 Ki.4:45, and Hosea 9:10. Jesus also used the fig tree as a metaphor for Israel's unfruitfulness in Luke 13:6 Mark 11:12-21. Then in Matt. 24:32 Jesus points to the fig tree/Israel as the way by which we may recognize the signs of the times. The Jews are back in their land, Israel is prosperous, and Jews are returning from around the world in record numbers. Are there any other signs that set this generation apart from any other time in history?

1. Man now has the capability of destroying the whole world. *"And unless those days were shortened, no flesh would be saved [survive],"* (Matthew 24:22).

2. We have the technology to prevent people from buying or selling any where in the world without proper identification as well as to track people down anywhere in the world, those who refuse the anti-christ's mark.. *"...and that no one may buy or sell except one who has the mark*

or the name of the beast, or the number of his name," (Revelation 13:17). Consider how our cell phones and computers give not only our location, but more personal information than we want to believe.

3. We can't help but notice the buildup of troops in Syria, Russia, Iran (Persia), and Turkey. These are the four main nations mentioned in Ezekiel 38 that will come against Israel from the north, (Syria is on Israel's northern border).

Please understand we are not basing our conclusion on figuring out numbers of days, blood moons, or convergence of planets, but rather on the fulfillment of the prophetic word of God. We realize that there will be those who will mock at the very concept of a "rapture," as if it is such a far-fetched, fanatical, and silly concept. Yet, people forget that the essence of our being, who we are as individuals, is much more software than it is hardware. What I mean is that the blueprint for every cell in our bodies is digitally encoded with a four letter alphabet (A,T,G, C) on our DNA. And not only do most people not bother to seriously consider **how** did that *digitally written information* get there, but WHO put it there. Letters are words and words are information and information denotes intelligence, not random chance. It is the most UNSCIENTIFIC idea to assert that such complexity of words and information were the result of a big bang; there is simply no explosion of any size that can produce order and information. While we upload movies, data, music, etc. every day and never give a thought to how that works, similarly the rapture is, in essence, a digital upload of the information which is the digitally coded identity of each believer. God Almighty wrote the code and God Almighty owns the information, and very soon is going to select, "upload My Church." People scoff at the truth of Creation, and they scoff at the truth of salvation, and they scoff at the truth of the rapture. God is not shocked and neither should we be. *"First of all, you must understand that in the last days scoffers will come, scoffing and following their own evil desires. They will say, 'Where is this 'coming' he promised? Ever since our fathers died, everything goes on as it has since the beginning of creation,"* (2 Peter 3:3-4, NIV).

Some will criticize you as one who wants to escape yet, Jesus taught the "escape" doctrine. *"Watch therefore, and pray always that you may be counted worthy to escape all these things that will come to pass, and to stand before the Son of Man"* (Luke 21:36). It is very significant to take note that there is a promised reward for those longing for His appearing. *"Finally, there is laid up for me the crown of righteousness, which the Lord, the righteous Judge, will give to me on that Day, and not to me only but also to all who have loved His appearing,"* (2 Timothy 4:8); *"So Christ was offered once to bear the sins of many. To those who eagerly wait for Him He will appear a second time, apart from sin, for salvation,"* (Hebrews 9:28). We are also instructed that those who are expecting His soon return should be motivated to obey and serve. *"Since everything will be destroyed in this way, what kind of people ought you to be? You ought to live holy and godly lives,"* (2 Peter 3:11, NIV). To paraphrase Peter, "Life is not about this life – Life is about the life to come!"

CHAPTER 8

The Seventh Seal
The First 4 Trumpets:
The One-Third Judgments

Keep in mind that of the seven trumpets of judgment only four are sounded in this chapter and are not to be mistaken with the trumpet referenced in either 1Corinthians 15:52 or 1 Thessalonians 4:16-18 as some get confused about. The trumpet mentioned in those portions of Scripture is not a trumpet of *judgment* from God but the trumpet, or *voice*, of God calling His Church out of this world.

Vs.1-6: *"When He opened the seventh seal, there was silence in heaven for about half an hour. And I saw the seven angels who stand before God, and to them were given seven trumpets. Then another angel, having a golden censer, came and stood at the altar. He was given much incense, that he should offer it with the prayers of all the saints upon the golden altar which was before the throne. And the smoke of the incense, with the prayers of the saints, ascended before God from the angel's hand. Then the angel took the censer, filled it with fire from the altar, and threw it to the earth. And there were noises, thunderings, lightnings, and an earthquake. So the seven angels who had the seven trumpets prepared themselves to sound."*

The opening of the seventh seal led to silence in heaven for about a half hour. Why is this so dramatic? Heaven is a place of continual rejoicing and song which is especially jubilant now that the rapture has occurred, and the Church is in the temple worshipping Yahweh with great rejoicing. Yet, now even Heaven itself is sobered and silenced as seven angels are given trumpets in anticipation of God's soon to commence judgment upon planet earth.

The angel with a golden censer who stands beside the altar is highlighted in our minds and we are reminded of the altar of incense which was in the Tabernacle in the wilderness where prayers to Yahweh were offered. In this case, the smoke of the incense along with the prayers of the saints ascends up to God from the angel's hand. How significant that as God's righteous judgment is about to commence the prayers of the saints is referenced first. The censer filled with incense and prayers now has fire added to it and is thrown to the earth. Now the silence has ended and there are noises, thunderings, lightnings, and an earthquake as all seven angels prepare themselves to sound in succession each of the seven trumpets of God's wrath. The seven years of tribulation on earth is about to commence. God has displayed His patience and restraint for approximately six thousand years and now His time of judgement has come.

We will find that even during the Tribulation God is ready to save as many as would receive Him. As I have shared many times before our God is a God of absolutely impartial love. His judgment does not negate nor suspend His great love, He is slow to anger and abounding in mercy, *"For I have no pleasure in the death of one who dies,' says the Lord God. 'Therefore turn and live!'"* (Ezekiel 18:32). However, if God does not bring judgment then His word is not only unreliable, it is untrue. If God does not judge the world then Adam and Eve should not have been cast out of the garden, the flood would have been unjust, and Jesus' substitutionary death on the cross was unnecessary.

Even in His wrath God makes room for salvation. There are many who have refused Christ that will be converted when the Tribulation begins. For many it will take the Tribulation to open their eyes. There are those who believe that those who rejected Christ before the Tribulation starts will not be able to accept Him once the Tribulation begins, or that only those who never heard the gospel will have the opportunity to be saved. However I believe such an idea is not only contrary to His nature but to his revealed will as found in 2 Pet.3:9. In fact I believe that during the Tribulation there will be one of the greatest revivals this planet has seen. There will be so many converts that the anti-Christ will have an entire system for identifying those who haven't taken his mark and for executing Tribulation saints. This should be a motivation for us to share our faith and make it known that we are anticipating the rapture. During the Tribulation sadly the vast majority do not repent but instead curse God even in the midst of the awesome display of His great and mighty power.

Vs.7: *"The first angel sounded: And hail and fire followed, mingled with blood, and they were thrown to the earth. And a third of the trees were burned up, and all green grass was burned up."*

With the sounding of the first trumpet there is hail, fire, and blood mingled together which are hurled to the earth. The Lord first brought world-wide judgment by water but now He is using fire just as we are informed in 2 Peter 3:7, and one third of the trees are burned up. The word rendered here, *green grass* is "khartos" (Gk) meaning *herbage*, or *vegetation*. All shrubbery, greenery, and vegetation will be gone. Burned. Consider the impact this will have on the people of earth. Plant life was the first to be created and will be the first to be destroyed (Genesis 1:11-13).

God created plant life after order was brought to the earth out of chaos, and now plants are destroyed when chaos comes on the earth.

Vs.8-9: *"Then the second angel sounded: And something like a great mountain burning with fire was thrown into the sea and a third of the sea became blood. And a third of the living creatures in the sea died, and a third of the ships were destroyed."*

When the second angel sounds his trumpet a massive object, "something like a great mountain," and which is burning with fire falls into the sea. The result is that one-third of the sea becomes blood, one-third of all the living creatures in the sea die, and one-third of the ships of all nations are destroyed. Take note that it does **not** say, *"something like"* one-third of the sea becomes blood, nor do we read, *"something like"* one-third of all the living creatures in the sea die, or that *"something like"* one-third of the ships of all nations are destroyed. Whatever this object is that falls into the sea with such catastrophic yet precisely measured devastation, I certainly do not believe that it is a missile of any kind. I believe it is nothing which man has made or could make but is something completely supernatural. The closest John can come to describing it is, *"something like a great mountain."* It is also interesting to note that in Creation, on the same day plant life appeared the Lord also separated the land from the sea (Genesis 1:9-10). Here in the case of

God's judgment plant life has been all but destroyed, and with the second trumpet judgment the sea is now devastated.

Vs.10-11: *"Then the third angel sounded: And a great star fell from heaven, burning like a torch, and it fell on a third of the rivers and on the springs of water. The name of the star is Wormwood. A third of the waters became wormwood, and many men died from the water, because it was made bitter."* *"Then the fourth angel sounded: And a third of the sun was struck, a third of the moon, and a third of the stars, so that a third of them were darkened. A third of the day did not shine, and likewise the night. And I looked, and I heard an angel flying through the midst of heaven, saying with a loud voice, Woe, woe, woe to the inhabitants of the earth, because of the remaining blasts of the trumpet of the three angels who are about to sound!"*

The Lord begins His judgement by touching the necessities of man: food, water, and natural light, all of which He provided in the first place. The world has denied the Creator and refused to give Him the praise and glory which is due Him, and now His gracious provisions are removed. With the sounding of the third trumpet a third of all the fresh water is made bitter.

Vs.12: *"Then the fourth angel sounded: And a third of the sun was struck, a third of the moon, and a third of the stars, so that a third of them were darkened. A third of the day did not shine, and likewise the night.*"

The fourth angel's trumpet blast leads to the darkening of the sun, moon, and stars. In other words, the wattage of all natural light is turned down by one third. Jesus said that He is the light of the world (Jn1:4; 8:12; 9:5). His light of life and truth has been rejected and so now the Lord God dims the natural light which He has so graciously provided since the dawn of creation. Ps 36:9, *"For with You is the fountain of life; In Your light we see light."* Ps 43:3-4 should be every believer's prayer and cry, *"Oh, send out Your light and Your truth! Let them lead me; Let them bring me to Your holy hill and to Your tabernacle. Then I will go to the altar of God, to God my exceeding joy; And on the harp I will praise You, O God, my God."* This judgment is interesting because a short time later the sun is given power to *scorch* the earth.

Vs.13: *"And I looked, and I heard an angel flying through the midst of heaven, saying with a loud voice, "Woe, woe, woe to the inhabitants of the earth, because of the remaining blasts of the trumpet of the three angels who are about to sound!"*

Subsequent to the first four trumpet blasts an angel flys through the midst of heaven crying out in a loud voice to pronounce woe upon the inhabitants of the earth in anticipation of the next three trumpets which are about to sound. Once again we see our loving

Creator God's plea and warning to mankind in order to give him opportunity to confess and repent. Imagine after having experienced the first four trumpets then hearing an angel sound this dire warning that the last three trumpet blasts will be much worse than what they have already suffered. This is why we cannot emphasize enough the need for people not to delay, but to turn their lives over to Christ, accepting His free gift of salvation. *"And do this, knowing the time, that now it is high time to awake out of sleep; for now our salvation is nearer than when we first believed. The night is far spent, the day is at hand. Therefore let us cast off the works of darkness, and let us put on the armor of light. Let us walk properly, as in the day, not in revelry and drunkenness, not in lewdness and lust, not in strife and envy. But put on the Lord Jesus Christ, and make no provision for the flesh, to fulfill its lusts,"* (Romans 13:11-14). This is a strong warning that we must not put off our salvation but ask the Lord Jesus Christ to take over our lives. If already a believer then to do the work of evangelism Christ has called us to. Otherwise, all those things we are reading about will befall those we have failed to share Christ with. This is by far the most sobering calling and responsibility there could ever be.

The first four trumpets were judgments on nature. Now, these last three are judgments that will be effected upon mankind himself, which explains why the angel gives such dire warning about the last three. These last three trumpets of the seven are called *the woe-trumpets.* Imagine the dread of the people on earth after all that has happened when they see an angel flying around crying in a loud voice, "Woe!"

Review Of Chapter 8:

v.7 – The First Trumpet: 1/3 of all Earth's vegetation has been destroyed.

vs 8-9 – The Second Trumpet: 1/3 of all sea creatures along with 1/3 of all ships in the sea have been destroyed.

vs10-11– The Third Trumpet: 1/3 of all fresh water has been rendered unusable.

vs12-13 –The Fourth Trumpet: 1/3 of the sun, moon and stars has been turned to darkness and 1/3 of the day and night are without light. An angel proclaims dire warning concerning the last three trumpets which are about to sound.

By this point there has no doubt already been a tremendous loss of human life, and in chapter 9:15 we are told that one-third of the world's remaining population will then also perish.

CHAPTER 9

THE FIFTH & SIXTH TRUMPETS:
THE BEGINNING OF WOES

Vs. 1-12: *"Then the fifth angel sounded: And I saw a star fallen from heaven to the earth. To him was given the key to the bottomless pit. And he opened the bottomless pit, and smoke arose out of the pit like the smoke of a great furnace. So the sun and the air were darkened because of the smoke of the pit. Then out of the smoke locusts came upon the earth. And to them was given power, as the scorpions of the earth have power. They were commanded not to harm the grass of the earth, or any green thing, or any tree, but only those men who do not have the seal of God on their foreheads. And they were not given authority to kill them, but to torment them for five months. Their torment was like the torment of a scorpion when it strikes a man. In those days men will seek death and will not find it; they will desire to die, and death will flee from them. The shape of the locusts was like horses prepared for battle. On their heads were crowns of something like gold, and their faces were like the faces of men. They had hair like women's hair, and their teeth were like lions' teeth. And they had breastplates like breastplates of iron, and the sound of their wings was like the sound of chariots with many horses running into battle. They had tails like scorpions, and there were stings in their tails. Their power was to hurt men five months. And they had as king over them the angel of the bottomless pit, whose name in Hebrew is Abaddon, but in Greek he has the name Apollyon. One woe is past. Behold still two more woes are coming after these."*

The fifth angel sounds his trumpet and immediately John sees a *"star fallen from heaven to earth"* (emphasis added). There's much debate regarding the identity of this "star" however I believe this is a celestial angel, not Satan, who is given the key to the bottomless pit. We can be certain of this because later on in chapter 20 an angel (I believe the same one, but it doesn't matter) who is already in possession of this key casts Satan into the pit, shuts him up and seals the pit for 1,000 years. At this point in chapter nine Satan isn't in the pit but is still *"roaming about like a roaring lion"* (1 Pet.5:8). He is however, the king of the demon locusts there. At the opening of the pit smoke like a great furnace pours out so much so that the sun and the air are darkened, and the locusts come out of the smoke.

This pit is understood to be the opening to Hell (*abyss* or *abussos*) and we must take note that although Satan is king of this dark domain he does not have the key! We are even told his name in two languages. Hebrew (Abaddon), and Greek (Apollyon) names which are aliases for Satan. Remember, Satan has not ever been sealed in the bottomless pit but has been free to go *"to and fro on the earth, and from walking back and forth on it,"* (Job 1:7 & 2:2).

A five-month long judgment of supernatural locusts ensues. The description of this horde is more terrifying than any Hollywood movie monster. This judgment will be so horrible that men will seek death but it will elude them. So much confusion has been generated needlessly by those who attempt to come up with a natural explanation for this demonic horde of locusts, asserting that they symbolize some kind of advanced military hardware. This is nonsense in my opinion. These locusts are a judgment from God and to try to wrap our finite minds around what is being described is futile. We marvel at the grace and mercy of God to the post-rapture saints who have the seal of God on their foreheads and are spared the torment of these supernatural locusts. God's love and grace are not removed when his church is removed from the world. There is more power in mercy than judgement.

Vs.13-19: *"Then the sixth angel sounded: And I heard a voice from the four horns of the golden altar which is before God, saying to the sixth angel who had the trumpet "Release the four angels who are bound at the great river Euphrates." So the four angels, who had been prepared for the hour and day and month and year, were released to kill a third of mankind. Now the number of the army of the horsemen was two hundred million; I heard the number of them. And thus I saw the horses in the vision: those who sat on them had breastplates of fiery red, hyacinth blue, and sulfur yellow; and the heads of the horses were like the heads of lions; and out of their mouths came fire, smoke, and brimstone. By these three plagues a third of mankind was killed — by the fire and the smoke and the brimstone which came out of their mouths. For their power is in their mouth and in their tails; for their tails are like serpents, having heads; and with them they do harm."*

When the sixth trumpet sounds John hears a voice from the four horns of the golden altar which is before God. Presumably the voice is God the Father's but we cannot say definitively. We are familiar with the golden altar because of the replica God gave Moses instructions to build in the wilderness. The voice John hears instructs the sixth angel who has the trumpet, to release four other angels who have been bound at the river Euphrates, and who have been prepared for this very hour and day and month and year. We know that these four angels are fallen angels (demons), not celestial angels, because they had been bound and are then released to kill one third of mankind. These angels seem especially destructive, and that is likely why they were bound. God's purposes are very exact. His timing is always perfect. The day these angels are released will be the exact year, month, day and hour the Lord had determined from the beginning.

The short book of Jude gives us an account of certain angels who were bound; whether or not it refers to these particular angels we do not know but it is certainly reasonable to conclude that they are simply because of what we are told in the last part of the verse, *"And the angels who did not keep their proper domain, but left their own abode, He has reserved in everlasting chains under darkness for the judgment of the great day,"* (Jude 1:6-7 emphasis added).

Why is it they were bound at the Euphrates River? We assert there is strong reason in that this is where the Garden of Eden was located, where human life began, where the first sin was committed, the first murder took place, the first war was fought, where the Flood began and spread over the earth and where the Tower of Babel was erected. Babylon was the fountainhead of idolatry and here is where these four angels have been held until this moment. It is horrible to think of one third of earth's population being destroyed by this judgment alone. The number of dead at this point would very likely be upward of one billion. It would be an impossible task to bury that many.

It is my opinion that this portion in Jude is referring to the incident in Genesis 6:1-4 when the unnatural union of fallen angels and human women produced the hybrid Nephilim. *"Now a population explosion took place upon the earth. It was at this time that beings from the spirit world looked upon the beautiful earth women and took any they desired to be their wives. Then Jehovah said, "My Spirit must not forever be disgraced in man, wholly evil as he is. I will give him 120 years to mend his ways." In those days, and even afterwards, when the evil beings from the spirit world were sexually involved with human women, their children became giants, of whom so many legends are told,"* (Genesis 6:1-4, TLB).

This completely unnatural union violated God's created order and the hybrid offspring which were produced were very likely violent and brutal beings. Without a doubt this shocking abnormality was in part what necessitated the world wide judgment of the Flood. God set a time frame of 120 years and it is interesting to note that 121 years after Genesis 6 the Flood came!

Here again we have an example of where the traditional view brings so much confusion and misunderstanding about Revelation. Many Bible believers today have been taught that this army is referencing the "kings of the east," mentioned in chapter 16, simply due to the number of 200 million, and also because the River Euphrates is also referred to in both portions. In addition, respected Bible teachers have asserted that this army is an earthly one, presumably Chinese simply due to the vast number (The United States at the time of this writing has a standing military of 21/2 million). However we must look at the context. This horde numbered in chapter nine is the result of the sixth ***trumpet.*** What is described in chapter sixteen is the result of the sixth ***bowl*** judgment. The very description of this army makes it abundantly clear by any rational thought that this army is not of this earth. Again, we must keep in mind that what mankind and the entire world system is experiencing are supernatural events which constitute the wrath of God. How preposterous to imagine that human riders could mount and direct the supernatural creatures which are described here as "horses." These are no ordinary, earthly horses and they most certainly are not any kind of military hardware no matter how advanced.

Vs.20-21: *"But the rest of mankind, who were not killed by these plagues, did not repent of the works of their hands, that they should not worship demons, and idols of gold, silver, brass, stone, and wood, which can neither see nor hear nor walk. And they did not repent of their murders or their sorceries or their sexual immorality or their thefts.*"

This portion is so astounding because it powerfully shows that no matter what they see the heart of mankind can be so full of pride that in blind defiance against all that is reasonable they refuse to turn to God. Men would rather suffer and die than to admit they are wrong, or that there is a Creator God whose very nature is Love. The words which the Lord spoke through the prophet Jeremiah so long ago are still relevant today, *"And the Lord has sent to you all His servants the prophets, rising early and sending them, but you have not listened nor inclined your ear to hear. They said, 'Repent now every one of his evil way and his evil doings, and dwell in the land that the Lord has given to you and your fathers forever and ever. Do not go after other gods to serve them and worship them, and do not provoke Me to anger with the works of your hands; and I will not harm you.' Yet you have not listened to Me,"* says the Lord, *"that you might provoke Me to anger with the works of your hands to your own hurt"* (Jer 25:4-7).

How tragic this is since the Lord has provided such a simple and powerful solution, *"The word is near you, in your mouth and in your heart (that is, the word of faith which we preach): that if you confess with your mouth the Lord Jesus and believe in your heart that God has raised Him from the dead, you will be saved.*

For with the heart one believes unto righteousness, and with the mouth confession is made unto salvation" . . . *"For whoever calls on the name of the Lord shall be saved"* (Rom. 10:8-10 & 13). How encouraging and assuring to know that believers have the promise of God that they will not experience His wrath. In this portion we have the sounding of the sixth trumpet and likely one of the worst judgements found in this prophetic book. It is beyond human understanding how any human being could experience these judgments on all the earth and not turn to the only one who can save them. In the same way, when we see how the world of our generation is deteriorating, we wonder why people aren't flocking to the Lord in droves.

CHAPTER 10

THE MIGHTY ANGEL AND THE LITTLE BOOK
THE SEVEN THUNDERS

This will be one of the shortest and yet one of the strangest chapters we cover, and yet so very profound.

Vs. 1-4: *"I saw still another mighty angel coming down from heaven, clothed with a cloud. And a rainbow was on his head, his face was like the sun, and his feet like pillars of fire. He had a little book open in his hand. And he set his right foot on the sea and his left foot on the land, and cried with a loud voice, as when a lion roars. When he cried out, seven thunders uttered their voices. Now when the seven thunders uttered their voices, I was about to write; but I heard a voice from heaven saying to me, Seal up the things which the seven thunders uttered, and do not write them."*

It is generally believed that this angel is Jesus Christ because of the similarities found in the description which John gives of Jesus in chapter 1:13-16. However I believe we have good reason to question that conclusion due to the fact that the angel described here swears to the Creator (vs.5-7). Jesus **is** the Creator of all things (John 1:1-5; Col.1:15-17) so my question is, if this angel is Christ why would he swear to Himself? I leave that to the reader to decide.

Notice that John understands whatever it is that the seven thunders have said and presumes that it is to be included in the prophetic message. However, John is told to seal up and not write what the voice of the thunders uttered. For most who read this portion, the mystery of the prophetic word of the seven thunders sparks deep curiosity. I have often wondered if perhaps the voice of the seven thunders will be unveiled to the Tribulation saints.

Vs.5-7: *"The angel whom I saw standing on the sea and on the land raised up his hand to heaven and swore by Him who lives forever and ever, who created heaven and the things that are in it, the earth and the things that are in it, and the sea and the things that are in it, that there should be delay no longer, but in the days of the sounding of the seventh angel, when he is about to sound, the mystery of God would be finished, as He declared to His servants the prophets."*

Once again it is reinforced that Yahweh is the Creator of all that exists, a fact which is clearly established from Genesis to this great book of Revelation. It defies all logic and all science to assert that anything (let alone the vast universe) can come from nothing, and so we understand, "In the beginning, GOD..." God created all things out of nothing because He preexisted all things and because He is eternally existent. Evolution is not based in any true, observable science. Evolution is a religion which takes much more faith to believe in simply because there is no evidence for it. Faith in Jesus Christ is based on irrefutable historical and archeological evidence.

We are now informed that when the seventh angel sounds his trumpet the mystery of God would be finished. Jesus told his disciples that to us it has been given to know *"the mystery of the kingdom of God,"* *(Matt. 4:11),* and we are informed in Romans 16:25 that the mystery (singular) of God which had been kept secret has now been made manifested by the prophetic Word. What is the "mystery of God?" Simply put, it is the Gospel message (Eph.6:19). However, we understand that there are several aspects to the singular "mystery of God" and these of course would include the mystery of the seven stars and the seven golden lampstands (Rev.1:20).

Here is a sampling of the facets of the mystery:

- That blindness in part has happened to Israel until every last Gentile who will be saved during the church age is saved (Rom. 11:25).

- The Rapture of the Church when the dead will be raised incorruptible and we who remain alive will be transformed and given immortal bodies (1 Cor. 15:51-54).
- That the will of God has been that He would gather together in one all things in Christ, both which are in heaven and which are on earth, and that the Gentiles should be fellow heirs with Jews. (Eph 1:10 & 3:3,4, & 9).

Read also Col.1:26 & 27; 2:2 and 4:3. I am not suggesting that this is a definitive answer to the entire meaning of "the mystery of God that is to be finished" but merely some thoughts to consider in its regard.

Vs 8-11: "*Then the voice which I heard from heaven spoke to me again and said, "Go, take the little book which is open in the hand of the angel who stands on the sea and on the earth." So I went to the angel and said to him, "Give me the little book. "And he said to me, "Take and eat it; and it will make your stomach bitter, but it will be as sweet as honey in your mouth." Then I took the little book out of the angel's hand and ate it, and it was as sweet as honey in my mouth. But when I had eaten it, my stomach became bitter. And he said to me, you must prophesy again about many peoples, nations, tongues, and kings.*"

I believe that John being told to "eat" the book is a metaphor for not only accepting the message, but also regarding his being re-commissioned to continue recording what he is being shown. Jeremiah and Ezekiel both used similar imagery, *"Your words were found, and I ate them, and Your word was to me the joy and rejoicing of my heart,"* (Jeremiah 15:16); *"Moreover He said to me, 'Son of man, eat what you find; eat this scroll, and go, speak to the house of Israel.' So I opened my mouth, and He caused me to eat that scroll. And He said to me, 'Son of man, feed your belly, and fill your stomach with this scroll that I give you.' So I ate, and it was in my mouth like honey in sweetness,"* (Ezekiel 3:1-3). Regardless of whether or not God's Word seems heavy or light, convicting or affirming, each believer should pray that God's word would be to us as it was to Job, *"I have treasured the words of His mouth more than my daily bread,"* (Job 23:12).

The "sweetness" of the book I believe very likely refers to the mystery of God being finished, and the fullness of all His promises coming to pass. The bitterness in his stomach could be the realization of the countless people who will suffer and die during the Tribulation although some will be saved. In addition the realization of the vast number of people who will continue to reject God's free gift of eternal life and be thrown into the Lake of Fire.

CHAPTER 11

THE TWO WITNESSES AND THE SEVENTH TRUMPET

Vs. 1-3: *"Then I was given a reed like a measuring rod. And the angel stood, saying, "Rise and measure the temple of God, the altar, and those who worship there. But leave out the court which is outside the temple, and do not measure it, for it has been given to the Gentiles. And they will tread the holy city underfoot for forty-two months."*

Carefully note that vs.1-6 are NOT the result of the sounding of a trumpet and so are not a judgment. These verses are simply the record of what John had been instructed to do and he is instructed not to measure the court which is "outside" because that has been "given to the Gentiles." *'The act of measuring indicates a separation between a portion which God recognizes: the Temple and worshipers, and what He rejects'* (biblestudytools.com). John is the one assigned to do the measuring and is told to measure the temple, the altar, and those who worship there. *'The temple and altar are to be literally measured whereas the presence of the worshipers is merely to be noticed and recorded. The verb measure "Zeugma" is by this figure 'yoked' to a second object which does not fit it as equally as the first, for worshippers would not be measured but taken account of."*

Daniel 9:27 informs us of a covenant or treaty which allows for sacrificial worship to be reinstituted and that the holy city Jerusalem would be occupied by Gentiles for 3½ years. Then, after 3½ years the daily sacrifices are brought to an end. I believe that quickly following the war of Ezek.38 a peace treaty is signed and a temple of sorts is built. Keep in mind that this temple will be nothing like Solomon's or Herod's in grandeur and in all likelihood will be erected relatively quickly following the war of Ezekiel 38. I believe that this temple will be more on the scale of the tabernacle in the wilderness. In my opinion it is plausible that this edifice may be temporary for the purpose of getting the daily sacrifices started right away, while a more permanent structure is being built upon which a wing (Dan.9:27) can be added. I've been asked, how would it be possible to build the third temple on the temple mount upon which the Dome of the Rock now sits? Up to this date if the Jews even attempt to set foot near the Dome of the Rock it causes an uprising among the Muslims. The answer to that dilemma will present itself following the war of Ezek.38. When those nations attack from the north all those armies are supernaturally destroyed by God. All the armies of Russia and most of the Muslim nations will be supernaturally obliterated by God. And so, simply stated, there will be no one left who would object to the temple being built. It is also possible that the Dome of the Rock is annihilated during the event.

Vs.4-6: *"These are the two olive trees and the two lampstands standing before the God of the earth. And if anyone wants to harm them, fire proceeds from their mouth and devours their enemies. And if anyone wants to harm them, he must be killed in this manner. These have power to shut heaven, so that no rain falls in the days of their prophecy; and they have power over waters to turn them to blood, and to strike the earth with all plagues, as often as they desire."*

Once again we find ourselves in prophetic territory that we cannot speak of in definite terms. Precisely how these events will unfold in detail we cannot know. However, we must keep in mind that Chapter eleven deals primarily with the death of the two witnesses, not their mission. Remember also that although we are only now coming to the place in John's written account where he is describing the death of the two witnesses, their <u>mission</u> has been going on for 3½ years. We know this because we are told in vs.3 that, *"they will prophesy one thousand two hundred and sixty days,"* but it is now in John's written account that their ministry is being brought to a violent end and there are yet another 3½ years of God's wrath to be poured out upon planet Earth.

The question is, who are these two witnesses, and what is their ministry of 'prophecy?' To answer the second part of the question we are told that, "The testimony of Jesus **is** the spirit of prophecy," Rev. 19:10. We are also told *"these are the two olive trees and the two lampstands standing before the God of the earth."* I believe these are the same *"two anointed ones, who stand beside the Lord of the whole earth,"* who were shown to Zechariah (Zech 4:14). In any case, we can be certain of the identity of one of them because the prophet Malachi foretold that Elijah would come, *"Behold, I will send you Elijah the prophet before the coming of the great and dreadful day of the Lord,* (Mal 4:5 emphasis added). Keep in mind, John the Baptist came in the *spirit* (Luke1:17). i.e. similar ministry of Elijah and was not Elijah himself. Scripture informs us that #1 *"It has been appointed for men to die* (permanently) only once and afterwards is judgment (Hebrews 9:27), and that #2- Elijah never experienced death but was *"taken up,"*(2 Kings 2:11). So then, it is my strong opinion based on Scripture that one of the witnesses here is the in the flesh prophet Elijah.

Many suppose the other witness to be Moses simply on the basis that some of the plagues which they are empowered by God to strike the earth with are similar to some of the plagues of Egypt. However I assert that it cannot be Moses due to the simple fact that Moses died. *"Moses was one hundred and twenty years old when he died,"* (Deuteronomy 34:6 & 7). In addition, consider the fact that saints of both the old and new testament who died have been resurrected and have met the Lord in the air "to <u>always</u>" be with Him (1 Thess. 4:17). At the rapture Moses, David, Abraham, were all translated to Heaven. On the other hand, there are only two people mentioned in the Bible that were "taken up" without having experienced death, Elijah and Enoch. *"And Enoch walked with God; and he was not (ya/yin;* gone, disappear), *for God took him (law/ ka/kh;* seize, to carry away)" (Genesis 5:24). *"By faith Enoch was <u>taken away so that he did not see death</u>, and was not found, because God had taken him; for before he was taken he had this testimony, that he pleased God,"* (Heb 11:5-6 emphasis added). With these two men, Enoch and Elijah, God has powerful witnesses from both the ante and post-diluvian times.

The majority of those living on the earth at this time will be utterly deceived by Satan and this world system, and will hate the two witnesses because they testify against their lawlessness. People don't hate Christianity and Christians simply because it is a religion they don't believe in; there are many religions. It is because Christians are filled with the Holy Spirit and the Spirit testifies against their lawlessness and convicts them of sin. In John 16:8-11 when Jesus promised to send the Holy Spirit He explained, *"And when He has come, He will convict the world of sin, and of righteousness, and of judgment: of sin, because they do not believe in Me; of righteousness, because I go to My Father and you see Me no more; of judgment, because the ruler of this world is judged."*

Vs. 7-10: *"Now when they finish their testimony, the beast that ascends out of the bottomless pit will make war against them, overcome them, and kill them. And their dead bodies will lie in the street of the great city which spiritually is called Sodom and Egypt, where also our Lord was crucified. Then those from the peoples, tribes, tongues, and nations will see their dead bodies three-and-a-half days, and not allow their dead bodies to be put into graves. And those who dwell on the earth will rejoice over them, make merry, and send gifts to one another, because these two prophets tormented those who dwell on the earth."*

We will address this beast who ascends out of the bottomless pit shortly. Until then we get a good picture of just how vicious the world has become against the testimony of God by how the people of earth respond to the death of the two witnesses. The death of the two witnesses apparently receives world -wide around the clock news coverage as people from every tribe, tongue, and nation see their dead bodies lying in the street for three-and-a-half days, and do not allow them to be buried. The world (what's left of it) rejoices in concert together over their death and actually celebrate it with gift giving. How bizarre and macabre. However, their jubilation is to be short lived. This *'beast that ascends out of the bottomless pit,'* is not to be confused with the beasts which ascend out of the sea and out of the earth in chapter 13. This beast is a demon entity which ascends *"out of the bottomless pit."*

Vs.11-14: *"Now after the three-and-a-half days the breath of life from God entered them, and they stood on their feet, and great fear fell on those who saw them. And they heard a loud voice from heaven saying to them, "Come up here." And they ascended to heaven in a cloud, and their enemies saw them. In the same hour there was a great earthquake, and a tenth of the city fell. In the earthquake seven thousand people were killed, and the rest were afraid and gave glory to the God of heaven. The second woe is past. Behold, the third woe is coming quickly."*

These precious servants of God are resurrected in full view of all the world and now raptured, having *"ascended to heaven in a cloud"*. Sound familiar?

We might not be the two witnesses of Revelation, but we are His witnesses now, and will also meet the Lord in the clouds, and there we shall be with Him forevermore. As we have already said, the world's euphoria over the death of these two saints is short lived. We must always remember that our trials, no matter how severe, are so very temporary and in the end, we are justified by faith in the Lord Jesus Christ. *"For our light affliction, which is but for a moment, is working for us a far more exceeding and eternal weight of glory, while we do not look at the things which are seen, but at the things which are not seen. For the things which are seen are temporary, but the things which are not seen are eternal. For we know that if our earthly house [referring to the physical body], this tent, is destroyed, we have a building from God, a house not made with hands, eternal in the heavens,"* (2 Cor 4:17-5:1).

At this point, the whole world has seen ample evidence that God's power is much greater than Satan's and should also realize that all the prophecies of the two witnesses will come to pass. Yet, most of the inhabitants of earth will still fail to repent. The division of the sheep and goats becomes more and more clear as the Tribulation progresses towards its culmination in Jesus' return to Earth to set up His Kingdom of righteousness. Some will repent and believe but sadly others will be filled with fear and rage. All of this has been the result of just the sixth trumpet's sounding.

Remember, we've been previously informed that, *"In the days of the sounding of the seventh angel,* ***when he is about to sound****, the mystery of God* *would be finished, as He declared to His servants the prophets,"*(Rev 10:7 emphasis added).

v.15-18 : *"Then the seventh angel sounded: And there were loud voices in heaven, saying, 'The kingdoms of this world have become the kingdoms of our Lord and of His Christ, and He shall reign forever and ever!' And the twenty-four elders who sat before God on their thrones fell on their faces and worshiped God, saying: 'We give You thanks, O Lord God Almighty, The One who is and who was and who is to come, Because You have taken Your great power and reigned. The nations were angry, and Your wrath has come, And the time of the dead, that they should be judged, And that You should reward Your servants the prophets and the saints, And those who fear Your name, small and great, And should destroy those who destroy the earth."*

Whenever I read this portion, I am awed by verse 16, *"And the twenty-four elders who sat before God on their thrones fell on their faces and worshiped God."* These are THE twenty-four elders we were introduced to in 4:1-5 and here they are still worshiping the Almighty! This verse really humbles me when I realize how superficial my worship is by comparison. At this point, the seventh angel sounds his trumpet to finish the mystery of God. All the earth will know the voice of God and the reality of the final judgment falling on the earth.

Vs 19: *"Then the temple of God was opened in heaven, and the ark of His covenant was seen in His temple. And there were lightnings, noises, thunderings, an earthquake, and great hail."*

Obviously what John is being shown here is not the replica of the ark, which Moses was instructed to build, but is the one and only original ark. It may be fun to speculate regarding the location of the ark Moses built, but what's important is that the original is right where it has always been. What else would we expect with such a disclosure but *"lightnings, noises, thunderings, an earthquake, and great hail."*

CHAPTER 12

WOMAN WITH THE MAN CHILD
THE RED DRAGON
WAR IN HEAVEN
WOMAN IN THE WILDERNESS

Make no mistake, the Book of Revelation continues to proceed chronologically. However in chapter 12:1-5 what John is shown is a highly condensed history of Israel and is the dividing point of the seven year Tribulation. Chapter 11 is the record of the death and resurrection of the two witness and the sounding of the seventh trumpet, and these two events concludes the first 31/2 years of the Tribulation period. We will find at the start of chapter 13 that the next 31/2 years of Tribulation continues uninterrupted with the arrival on the scene of the beast which arises out of the sea, and beast which arises out of the earth. Also during the last 31/2 years Israel is hidden away in the wilderness where she is supernaturally protected by God.

Vs.1-5 : *"Now a great sign appeared in heaven: a*

woman clothed with the sun, with the moon under her feet, and on her head a garland of twelve stars. Then being with child, she cried out in labor and in pain to give birth. And another sign appeared in heaven: behold, a great, fiery red dragon having seven heads and ten horns, and seven diadems on his heads. His tail drew a third of the stars of heaven and threw them to the earth, and the dragon stood before the woman who was ready to give birth, to devour her child as soon as it was born. She bore a male Child who was to rule all nations with a rod of iron. And her Child was caught up to God and His throne".

Verses 1-2 is a depiction of the vision given to Joseph in Gen.37:9 which was a prophecy of the future nation of Israel. In verses 3-4 John is shown a depiction of the rebellion and expulsion of Satan from heaven as well as his attempt to kill the woman's Child. At v erse 5 we read of Jesus' future rule over the nations and of His resurrection to the throne of God. This Child can only be Jesus Christ who alone gave His life as atonement for sin, was buried, and rose again. Only Jesus can and will *rule all nations with a rod of iron,*" (Ps.2:8; Rev.2:27). We are told that these details, which sometimes believers take for granted, are a 'great' <u>*sign*</u> not a metaphor or symbol. This demonstrates to us that the entire book of Revelation is to be understood literally. In addition consider that we are informed that the dragon was standing ready to devour the woman's child the moment he is born and we know that not only did Satan attempt to destroy Jesus from the moment he was born (Matthew 2:16) and failed, but he also many times tried to prevent Messiah from ever being born by inspiring programs to genocide the Jews, as in Esther chapters 3-4.

Verses 3-6 of this chapter are some of the most interesting verses in this book of prophecy. This fiery red dragon without question is Satan and the third of the stars that his tail sweeps from heaven to earth are his fallen angels, those who followed Satan in his rebellion against God and His throne. The woman who euphemistically had the Child is the nation Israel which God promises to protect for the last half of the Tribulation. This group of Jews will have a significant part in the Millennial Kingdom when Jesus returns with His Church.

This fiery red dragon is clearly identified as Satan himself later on in verse nine. Because of his treachery and rebellion Satan lost the exalted office given to him by God which he once held in Heaven, possibly as the worship leader (Ezek. 28:13-15). *"How you are fallen from heaven, O Lucifer, son of the morning! How you are cut down to the ground, you who weakened the nations,"* (Isa 14:12-15). Satan's three "I wills" of defiance described by the prophet Isaiah were so persuasive that he was able to draw one third of the angels into his rebellion with him and they then became the *fallen* angels, and also lost their place in Heaven. Not only 1/3 of the angels followed Satan, but so has all the world (1John 5:19).

Almost all commentators agree the Child here is Jesus, the Messiah. Some quarters which have been misled by replacement theology erroneously assert that the Child is the church [and that is not the only serious and grievous error of replacement theology]. Simply put, the church was never prophesied to rule the nations with an iron scepter. None other than Jesus Christ is going to accomplish that (See Psalm 2:9; 22:28; Rev. 2:27 and 19:11-16).

Vs.6- "*Then the woman fled into the wilderness, where she has a place prepared by God, that they should feed her there one thousand two hundred and sixty days.*"

There are three differing views as to the identity of the Woman mentioned here and in verses 1-2. The confusion is both unnecessary and unfortunate, and is the result of regarding portions such as the one before us as being merely symbolic and failing to recognize the very real historical reference. For example, the Roman Catholic Church asserts that the woman is Mary, and both Dominion as well as Replacement theologies assert that the woman is the Church. However if we allow scripture to be the best commentary on scripture, and with a view of the context of this portion, the most logical and common sense view is that the woman is the nation Israel who "gave birth" to Messiah, who was caught up to God and His throne. Consider, for example: 1) The woman is cared for <u>during the Tribulation</u>, which eliminates Mary who took part in the rapture. 2) The Church has been raptured and so is also eliminated as being identified as the woman. In addition, neither can the woman be properly identified as the Tribulation saints because we are told that rather than being divinely protected, the Tribulation saints are pursued and overtaken by anti-Christ: *"It was granted to him to make war with the saints and to overcome them,"* (Revelation 13:7).

The children of God will face such extreme persecution that two thirds of them will be put to death by the son of perdition (2Thess 2:3,4). By chapter 12 Satan has been cast out of heaven and is in an uncontrollable state of anger and rage knowing his time is short. *"'And it shall come to pass in all the land,' Says the Lord, 'That two-thirds in it shall be cut off and die, But one-third shall be left in it: I will bring the one-third through the fire,"* (Zechariah 13:8-9). *"And so all Israel will be saved, as it is written,"* (Romans 11:26). This portion in Romans is affirming that the fulfillment of Zechariah 13:8-9 is without doubt. The remaining one third Jews will all come to know Christ as their Messiah. Shortly we will see that God protects them from Satan. The place where the nation of Israel (the Woman) will flee to is in all likelihood Petra which is located in Jordan. Petra was the capital of Edom, and is situated 170 miles southwest of Amman, and about 50 miles south of the Dead Sea. 'Petra' which means *rock* is not mentioned in the Bible by that name but is called, *Bozrah* and *Sela.* This 'woman' from verses 1-6 and again later in verses 13-17 is the nation Israel and she represents the promise which God gave to the Jews that once He had regathered them to their land, they would never cease to be a nation. *"Thus says the Lord, Who gives the sun for a light by day, the ordinances of the moon and the stars for a light by night, Who disturbs the sea, and its waves roar (The Lord of hosts is His name):* '*If those ordinances depart from before Me, says the Lord, then the seed of Israel shall also cease from being a nation before Me forever,"* (Jeremiah 31:35-36). Therefore, we know that the ones protected in the wilderness by the Lord are the remaining one third of Israel's population, those who have recognized Jesus Christ as their Messiah and Savior.

Vs.7-9: *"And war broke out in heaven: Michael and his angels fought with the dragon; and the dragon and his angels fought, but they did not prevail, nor was a place found for them in heaven any longer. So the great dragon was cast out, that serpent of old, called the Devil and Satan, who deceives the whole world;*

he was cast to the earth, and his angels were cast out with him."

We know from the book of Job that Satan had access to Heaven and there he accused the brethren. Now however, he is being denied that access. These verses give us a little more detail on verse three and describe Satan's final and absolute expulsion from Heaven. We know from Job 1:6-7 and 2:1 that Satan and his followers presented themselves before God apparently on a regular basis. The phrase rendered in these verses *'sons of God'* is *bne-elohim* (Heb) or 'angels', as in the fallen variety of Jude 6. Now Satan is denied the access by which he has accused the brethren, of which Job is the supreme example. *"Nor was a place found for them in heaven any longer."*

Vs.10-11: *"Then I heard a loud voice saying in heaven, "Now salvation, and strength, and the kingdom of our God, and the power of His Christ have come, for the accuser of our brethren, who accused them before our God day and night, has been cast down. And they overcame him by the blood of the Lamb and by the word of their testimony, and they did not love their lives to the death."*

These voices echo the chorus of loud voices in chapter 11:15-16, *"And there were loud voices in heaven, saying, "The kingdoms of this world have become the kingdoms of our Lord and of His Christ, and He shall reign forever and ever!"* From the very beginning God's will has been a done deal.

Vs. 12-13: *"Therefore rejoice, O heavens, and you who dwell in them! Woe to the inhabitants of the earth and the sea! For the devil has come down to you, having great wrath, because he knows that he has a short time. Now when the dragon saw that he had been cast to the earth, he persecuted the woman who gave birth to the male Child."*

What Heaven rejoices over, Satan being cast out, is cause for woe to earth dwellers. Satan will direct the full force of his hatred for God at the ones God loves.

Vs.14-16: *"But the woman was given two wings of a great eagle, that she might fly into the wilderness to her place, where she is nourished for a time and times and half a time, from the presence of the serpent. So the serpent spewed water out of his mouth like a flood after the woman, that he might cause her to be carried away by the flood. But the earth helped the woman, and the earth opened its mouth and swallowed up the flood which the dragon had spewed out of his mouth."*

What these verses are describing and exactly how Israel will be protected I personally do not believe we can understand from our point in time. However, we know that God has already supernaturally preserved the nation Israel against insurmountable odds since 1948 and will continue to do so, because God always keeps His Word (Jer.31:35-36).

Vs.17: *"And the dragon was enraged with the woman, and he went to make war with the rest of her offspring, who keep the commandments of God and have the testimony of Jesus Christ."*

God's people continue to be Satan's favorite target, not just believing Jews, but the gentiles who come to faith during the Tribulation. As I mentioned earlier, I believe the greatest revival the world has ever seen will be during the Tribulation. Satan hates with a passion those who love God.

We will find that Satan will heighten his attempts to imitate the things of God, because he knows there is no one higher to imitate. We are instructed in 2 Cor 11:14-15 that, *"Satan himself transforms himself into an angel of light. Therefore it is no great thing if his ministers also transform themselves into ministers of righteousness, whose end will be according to their works." "The coming of the lawless one is according to the working of Satan, with all power, signs, and lying wonders, and with all unrighteous deception among those who perish,"* (2 Thess 2:9-10).

Have you ever wondered why it is only Jesus' name that people all over the world take in vain, and profane? Consider, have you ever heard anyone stub their toe, drop a glass, spill something, or break something and yell, "Oh Buddah" or, "Hare Krishna." Or ever ask the false god Vishnu to condemn something or someone? I am being totally serious here. People of every religion and even atheists only use Jesus' name as a curse word. Why is that do you suppose? I can tell you with absolute certainty it is because Satan's desire is to make that name *"which is above every name"* and the name at which *"every knee should bow"* (Phil.2:9-11) the most common and debase name used as a swear word. The name of Jesus is the ultimate reality as He said, "I Am the Truth," (John 14:6). It is only by Jesus' name that we can and must be saved. *"And she will bring forth a Son, and you shall call His **name Jesus**, for He will save His people from their sins,"* (Matt 1:21 emphasis added). *"Nor is there salvation in any other, for there is **no other name** under heaven given among men by which we must be saved,"* (Acts 4:12 emphasis added). *"For there is one God and one Mediator between God and men, the Man Christ **Jesus**, who gave Himself a ransom for all, to be testified in due time,"* (Tim 2:5-6 emphasis added). Jesus himself said, *"I am the way, the truth, and the life. No one comes to the Father except through Me,"* (John 14:6 emphasis added).

Remember, Satan's fall was due to his great pride and in his twisted psyche he has convinced himself that he is as great or greater than God, and by deceit and cunning he has convinced many others to join him in his delusion.

REVIEW: In our study, we have now come to the middle of the Tribulation: The Two Witnesses prophecied for the first three and a half years, while the anti-Christ pursues and persecutes believers on earth for the last three and a half years. This portion is the dividing point between the first and second half of the Tribulation. The remnant of believing Israel are protected for the last three and a half years as the anti-Christ goes on a rampage to persecute believing Israel and the rest of her children, referring to gentiles who get saved.

CHAPTER 13

THE LAST 3½ YEARS BEGIN; THE BEAST FROM THE SEA AND THE BEAST FROM THE EARTH

At this point the Tribulation is half over and we are introduced to two beasts: one from the sea, the other from the earth and so we clearly understand that the anti-christ had not yet come to power before this point. We will find with careful study that the beast out of the sea is not initially referring to any individual *person*, but rather a *government system* which is under the complete control of Satan. This tyrannical, idolatrous government system permeates and has authority over every facet of life. There is no doubt that we already are presently living in a world system that is utterly corrupt and opposed to Jesus. As is true today, being ruled by Jesus Christ is the one and only alternative to being ruled by the world system. Jesus prayed for believers that although they would have to live <u>in</u> the world yet they would not be <u>of</u> the world (Jn.17:14-16).

The Beast Out Of The Sea:

Vs.1-4: *"Then I stood on the sand of the sea. And I saw a beast rising up out of the sea, having seven heads and ten horns, and on his horns ten crowns, and on his heads a blasphemous name. Now the beast which I saw was like a leopard, his feet were like the feet of a bear, and his mouth like the mouth of a lion. The dragon gave him his power, his throne, and great authority. And I saw one of his heads as if it had been mortally wounded, and his deadly wound was healed. And all the world marveled and followed the beast. So they worshiped the dragon who gave authority to the beast; and they worshiped the beast, saying, 'Who is like the beast? Who is able to make war with him?'"*

This is an obvious example of when symbolism is used in Revelation. This confederation of nations was also shown to Daniel depicted as a leopard, bear, and lion (7:5-8). This is how God sees these nations, as brute beasts. The fierceness of the last beast which Daniel sees likely refers to the beast, or anti-christ, because it has ten horns and particularly that the little horn which becomes prominent among the others has a mouth which speaks pompous words.

I believe that beast #1 which rises up out of the sea is not a demonic being or an individual, but represents a tightly knit confederation of 7 nation states and so it is seen as a single "beast". The 'heads' are the leaders of each state, the 'horns' depict their power and the 'crowns' their authority which we are told has come from Satan himself. This beast has seven heads, ten horns and ten crowns but one blasphemous name. Take note that it is <u>one</u> of the seven heads which receives a mortal wound and this wound is supernaturally healed which incites the whole world to marvel and to follow after "<u>the beast</u>". Then they worship Satan because he gave authority to the beast, and they worship the beast too saying, '*who is like the beast*'. We will discover later on that the head that was mortally wounded and healed eventually absorbs the other six and rules alone as the anti-christ, or *the beast*. The second beast will set up an image of this first beast and require that he be worshipped.

Vs.5-8: "*And he was given a mouth speaking great things and blasphemies, and he was given authority to continue for forty-two months* (3½ yrs). *Then he opened his mouth in blasphemy against God, to blaspheme His name, His tabernacle, and those who dwell in heaven. It was granted to him to make war with the saints and to overcome them. And authority was given him over every tribe, tongue, and nation. All who dwell on the earth will worship him, whose names have not been written in the Book of Life of the Lamb slain from the foundation of the world.*"

The fact that we are told here that the beast is given authority for 42 months is clear evidence that he doesn't come into power until halfway through the Tribulation, because he is active in world affairs until the end. There will be a God-hating world, and this is the God-hating world government influenced and run by Satan which will produce the anti-Christ leader. Satan needs a physical man, a false messiah, to carry out his final solution against the followers of God. This anti-Christ will not only blaspheme God, but His temple and His chosen people as well, and will have victory over the tribulation saints. The only humans on earth who will not worship the beast will be those whose names are written in the Book of Life, in other words those who have become believers.

Vs. 9-10: *"If anyone has an ear, let him hear. He who leads into captivity shall go into captivity; he who kills with the sword must be killed with the sword. Here is the patience and the faith of the saints."*

Here we are reminded of the same phrase which closed every letter to the churches. God calls for the patience and the faith of the saints to submit to and trust in the sovereign and perfect will of God. He alone knows the timing and means of our departure from this life, and there is comfort for these Tribulation saints to know that God will avenge their suffering. When the sword comes out of Jesus' mouth to destroy anti-Christ, he and his partners will be thrown into the Lake of Fire. Also, here we have echoed the admonition of Hebrews 6:12 *"And we desire that each one of you show the same diligence to the full assurance of hope until the end, that you do not become sluggish, but imitate those who through faith and patience inherit the promises.*" The patience and faith of the saints of every age has been to diligently cling to the assurance of hope that is found in Jesus Christ alone, *"For whatever is born of God overcomes the world. And this is the victory that has overcome the world — our faith,"* (1 John 5:4).

The Beast Out Of The Earth:

Vs.11-18: *"Then I saw another beast coming up out of the earth, and he had two horns like a lamb and spoke like a dragon. And he exercises all the authority of the first beast in his presence, and causes the earth and those who dwell in it to worship the first beast, whose deadly wound was healed. He performs great signs, so that he even makes fire come down from heaven on the earth in the sight of men. And he deceives those who dwell on the earth by those signs which he was granted to do in the sight of the beast, telling those who dwell on the earth to make an image to the beast who was wounded by the sword and lived. He was granted power to give breath to the image of the beast, that the image of the beast should both speak and cause as many as would not worship the image of the beast to be killed. He causes all, both small and great, rich and poor, free and slave, to receive a mark on their right hand or on their foreheads, and that no one may buy or sell except one who has the mark or the name of the beast, or the number of his name. Here is wisdom. Let him who has understanding calculate the number of the beast, for it is the number of a man: his number is 666."*

It seems apparent that by this point the coalition of seven heads, ten horns and ten crowns have been assimilated into the personage of the beast which came up out of the sea because here the deadly wound which was healed is attributed directly to the beast rather than to one of the heads. Although this second beast has all the authority of the first, he is apparently willing to take the position of Vice Beast, if you will. It appears that this second beast is more of an enforcer for the first beast and is the one who puts into effect the following dark policies:

- Causes the Earth to worship the first beast
- Performs great signs to deceive the whole earth
- Requires that an image of the first beast be built
- Is granted power to give breath to the image so that it can not only speak but can also kill any who are non-compliant.
- Causes all to receive a mark without which they can neither buy nor sell.

His appearance will be very serene and gentle, but his words and actions will be vicious and brutal. Keep in mind that Satan was the one who gave the first beast his power, throne and authority. Now we are beginning to see the emergence of the person who is commonly known as the false prophet (Rev.16:3; 19:20; 20:10). Also note that the term, *anti*-Christ can mean 'against,' but it can also mean *in place of.* This anti-Christ will be against Christ by claiming to be Christ. We see how this false prophet will counterfeit the work of the Holy Spirit by placing his seal on unbelievers, sealing them for the day of judgement. His mark is 666 the number of a man. On the contrary, the Holy Spirit has sealed every believer for the day of redemption (Eph.1:13). Remember, the focus of the second beast is to force all to worship the first beast as he moves the world population from a political agenda to a spiritual one.

Satan has always used lying signs and wonders to deceive man. *"The coming of the lawless one is according to the working of Satan, with all power, signs, and lying wonders, and with all unrighteous deception among those who perish, because they did not receive the love of the truth, that they might be saved. And for this reason God will send them strong delusion, that they should believe the lie,"* (2 Thessalonians 2:9-11). God has provided in His word ample warning regarding this delusion. Keep in mind when Jesus was asked to perform a sign He said, "*A wicked and adulterous generation seeks after a sign, and no sign shall be given to it except the sign of the prophet Jonah,*" (Matthew 16:4). Remember all the wonders and miracles Jesus performed were so that people might believe the truth, and recognize that He was the fulfillment of all of the Messianic prophecies. In contrast, these signs performed by the second beast on behalf of the first are all for the purpose of deception. Consider, God always reveals while Satan always deceives; God is Love and Satan is hate. The Lord is gracious and compassionate (Ex.34:6; Ps. 145:8,9) whereas Satan holds the ominous titles of *destroyer* and *deceiver.* He is using lying signs and wonders today to deceive, just as he has from the beginning of time, because he hates God and His special creation. Consider how many churches are caught up in every latest program, trend, and movement but do not emphasize the great need for the study of God's Word and for prayer.

The most dangerous and deadly deceptions are those that most closely resemble the truth. This is why Jesus commanded us not to be deceived. Remember, the anti-Christ will deceive all by pretending to be Christ. He is not going to go around saying, "I am the son of the Devil," no, he will be deceiving people into thinking he is the son of God.

This false prophet, the second beast, tells those who

dwell on the earth to make an image to the beast. When we consider the daily advancements in technology it's not much of a challenge to think that this image could probably be made today. AI technology today can not only speak but even respond to the human voice. Because we are specifically told that the second beast is "granted power" to give <u>breath</u> to the image, I strongly believe that it will be a demonic, supernatural creation and not simply a technological or manufacturing marvel. The image itself isn't a far-fetched idea, but the thought of it being given breath and empowered to both speak and to kill is terrifying. It is of course Satan who instigates this entire program. Since his initial rebellion against God, Satan has lusted after the worship and adoration which rightly only belongs to Jesus. That is why he feverishly pushes that the image be worshiped. Here, the word for worship is *proskooneho,* and can be used for both worship in the religious sense or in the sense of civil homage as to a king or leader, which is the case here, as it is proceeded by the word *poy-eh-o* 'causes' or *forces.* However, I do not believe that the beast's identification program is actually put into effect at this point. Programs of such a scale and scope cannot be immediately implemented, but people are informed and usually there is a date set at which time it is to begin (Read Esther chapter 3-4). Remember, the only alternative to worshiping the image is death. At that time the greatest persecution of Christians the world has ever seen will occur and it will make the Inquisition pale in comparison.

<u>Vs.18</u>: *"Here is wisdom. Let him who has understanding calculate the number of the beast, for it is the number of a man: his number is 666."*

Many have attempted to explain what the number 666 means and have filled books with speculation. There is a seeming paradox here because we are told to 'calculate the number of the beast' and then we are told what his number is. However I believe the meaning of the number is a mystery to us now for the same reason Daniel was told to seal up the vision he was given, it was meant for the end of the age (Daniel 8:26). I believe that when the time comes, people will know exactly who this man is and exactly what his number means.

CHAPTER 14

3 Angels
144,000 In Heaven,
Christ Reaps The Harvest of
the Tribulation Saints

Here, in chapter 14 verses 1-5, we have an intermission in John's taking dictation of events which are transpiring on the earth, and he is shown what is going on in Heaven. However, be aware **that there is no interruption in the events taking place on earth.** We are merely being given a glimpse of events in Heaven. Take note that there are other such intermissions in later chapters as well, and these usually precede something new which is about to commence on earth.

Vs.1-5: *"Then I looked, and behold, a Lamb standing on Mount Zion, and with Him one hundred and forty-four thousand, having His Father's name written on their foreheads. And I heard a voice from heaven, like the voice of many waters, and like the voice of loud thunder. And I heard the sound of harpists playing their harps. They sang as it were a new song before the throne, before the four living creatures, and the elders; and no one could learn that song except the hundred and forty-four thousand who were redeemed from the earth. These are the ones who were not defiled with women, for they are virgins. These are the ones who follow the Lamb wherever He goes. These were redeemed from among men, being first fruits to God and to the Lamb. And in their mouth was found no deceit, for they are without fault before the throne of God."*

The 144,000 which were sealed in chapter seven have arrived in Heaven. We aren't told if they were martyred or raptured, but in any case they have now taken their place right beside the Lamb. They have been set apart and are honored by being given a song which no one else can learn. At this point their work on earth has been completed, and in the meantime one third of all the Jews on earth have come to know Jesus as their Messiah and will be hidden away, out of the hands of the anti-Christ until the end of the Tribulation.

There is a lot of activity in vs. 6-12, three different angels fly in the midst of Heaven; the first angel proclaims the everlasting gospel, the second angel announces the fall of Babylon, and the third angel issues a dire warning.

Vs.6-12: *"Then I saw another angel flying in the*

midst of heaven, having the everlasting gospel to preach to those who dwell on the earth—to every nation, tribe, tongue, and people—saying with a loud voice, 'Fear God and give glory to Him, for the hour of His judgment has come; and worship Him who made heaven and earth, the sea and springs of water.' "And another angel followed, saying, 'Babylon is fallen, is fallen, that great city, because she has made all nations drink of the wine of the wrath of her fornication.' Then a third angel followed them, saying with a loud voice, 'If anyone worships the beast and his image, and receives his mark on his forehead or on his hand, he himself shall also drink of the wine of the wrath of God, which is poured out full strength into the cup of His indignation. He shall be tormented with fire and brimstone in the presence of the holy angels and in the presence of the Lamb. And the smoke of their torment ascends forever and ever; and they have no rest day or night, who worship the beast and his image, and whoever receives the mark of his name. Here is the patience of the saints; here are those who keep the commandments of God and the faith of Jesus."

With the witness and testimony of the 144,000 along with the two witnesses having been completed, we now come to the last agent of evangelism to the world. The first angel flying in the midst of heaven preaching the everlasting gospel and confirming again God as Creator of heaven and earth. The Lord never allows the world to be without a voice for Him for even Creation itself has testified of His glory and power (Romans 1:20-21). This angel's message is the fulfillment of Matthew 24:14, *"And this gospel of the kingdom will be preached in all the world as a witness to all the nations, and then the end will come."* Also, he is flying in "the midst of" what is known as 'the first heaven,' meaning our atmosphere. That the people of earth hear the first angel's proclamation indicates it was issued within clear range of being heard. As I mentioned earlier, all mankind will be without excuse. It is so hard to imagine that the hardness of men's hearts is to such an extent that an angel can be flying in midair proclaiming the eternal gospel, and they refuse to receive it. It is the <u>everlasting</u> gospel. It has not changed and it is non- negotiable. The Lord has always given warning of His judgments through His prophets, and in this case through His angels.

When the first angel finishes preaching the everlasting gospel, a second angel follows to announce that the great city Babylon has fallen. Then a third angel issues a stern warning given to those who would take the mark of the beast and/or worship his image. And so we understand clearly that mark of the beast has not been instituted before this point because otherwise the angel's warning would be after the fact.

There are three aspects to the 'Babylons' mentioned in the book of Revelation: Commercial/Financial

Babylon (here and chap 18), Political Babylon (16:9), and Religious Babylon (17:5). Each aspect of Babylon had its inception in the rebellion of man and was first organized by Nimrod when the people of earth endeavored to, *"build themselves a great city,"* in direct defiance to God's revealed will that they spread abroad (Gen.10:9 & 11:4). I believe it is the commercial/financial aspect of Babylon being referenced here, specifically Wall Street in New York City. People who don't know God and are unaware of His great plan of salvation live for money and pleasure, so when the worlds' financial system goes down there will be great mourning. The financial loss will be such as the world has never seen before. The "fall of Babylon" is progressive as we will discover in chapter 18.

We should clearly understand that no one is going to be fooled into taking the mark although the only alternative will be to be put to death by the image. However, the warning about anti-Christ has been abundant and clear, and men will be without excuse when they stand before the Lord.

Vs.13: *"Then I heard a voice from heaven saying to me, 'Write: Blessed are the dead who die in the Lord from now on.' 'Yes,' says the Spirit, 'that they may rest from their labors, and their works follow them."*

Death is not feared by believers. The propitiatory death of Jesus Christ and His resurrection has removed the sting of death (1 Cor.15:54-57), and His unconditional love, mercy, and grace, along with His exceedingly great and precious promises has removed all fear (1John 4:18). Those believers who die in the Lord from this point on will escape the devastation and suffering yet to come upon the world, and will find themselves in the presence of the Lord for all eternity. We cannot even imagine what the mind-set of these believers would be after all they've survived up to this point. I can't help but think that after the church was raptured that perhaps many, many people found access to a Bible and read this great book of prophecy. Read ahead to chapter 20:4 to understand what their perspective would be if they did.

Just as a side note: no matter how rich, successful, strong, popular, or even well-connected you are the day is coming when you will die. At that point, the amount of money you have, the number of relationships you have had, how many people agreed with your politics, all these matters of life will not matter at all. The only thing that will matter is if your name is written in the Lamb's Book of Life. All of your earthly accomplishments and activities will mean nothing if you are not His. Put simply, there is nothing more important than your eternal soul.

Vs.14-16: *"Then I looked, and behold, a white cloud, and on the cloud sat One like the Son of Man, having on His head a golden crown, and in His hand a sharp sickle. And another angel came out of the temple, crying with a loud voice to Him who sat on the cloud, "Thrust in Your sickle and reap, for the time has come for You to reap, for the harvest of the earth is ripe." So He who sat on the cloud thrust in His sickle on the earth, and the earth was reaped."*

Here we see another example of where symbolism is used in Revelation with the terms "sickle" and "reaping" to describe the rapture of all those who have been saved up to this point. I believe these are the very same who we read of in verses 2-3 of the next chapter. Take note that we are told that the earth was reaped indicating this reaping will be worldwide. These believers are raptured and thus spared the remaining bowl judgments. This harvest is ripe, as the tribulation saints have endured hardships that have not been seen since the first century. They have exercised patience and faith and have endured to the end and therefore will inherit the promises (Heb.6:12). We must understand that the Resurrection began with Jesus Christ, He being the first to rise and be glorified (Acts 26:23 & 1 Cor.15:20-23). The Rapture of His church as well as this 'reaping' of the saints are also part of the first Resurrection. All of the unsaved who have died will not be raised to face judgment until after the 1,000 year reign of Jesus Christ is completed.

Vs.17-20: *"Then another angel came out of the temple which is in heaven, he also having a sharp sickle. And another angel came out from the altar, who had power over fire, and he cried with a loud cry to him who had the sharp sickle, saying, 'Thrust in your sharp sickle and gather the clusters of the vine of the earth, for her grapes are fully ripe.' So the angel thrust his sickle into the earth and gathered the vine of the earth, and threw it into the great winepress of the wrath of God. And the winepress was trampled outside the city, and blood came out of the winepress, up to the horses' bridles, for one thousand six hundred furlongs."*

Here in these closing verses of chapter 14 we have more angelic activity. However, this action is the polar opposite of that which Jesus conducted in verse fourteen. Jesus <u>reaps</u> the tribulation saints up to glory; this angel <u>gathers</u> the *unbelievers* to be subject to the coming bowl judgments. The fruit of the sin and rebellion promoted by the world system, which has been cultivated by the people of earth for thousands of years, has now come to full bloom and we are about to see the culmination of what the earth has sown.

The precise measurement of the blood which is given (aprox. 200 miles) is another example of when symbolism is used in Revelation and I believe is an indication of the severity of the coming bowl judgments and the staggering death toll which will result. All this is preparation for what we read in the next chapter. Almighty God has done everything for man so that this need not have happened, but in justice and love, He must exact judgment on those who have been in league with Satan's treacherous agenda against the Lord and against His Anointed one, Jesus Christ.

CHAPTER 15

SEVEN ANGELS GIVEN THE SEVEN LAST JUDGMENTS; TRIBULATION SAINTS SING THE SONG OF MOSES

Chapter fifteen in its entirety is the scene in Heaven and is the prelude to the bowl judgements of God when the seven angels receive their golden bowls of wrath to pour out on the earth, which we are informed will complete the wrath of God. God's plan is perfect from eternity past. It is extremely significant, seven being the number of completion, that it is seven seals which conclude the record mankind's history up to the rapture, and seven trumpets which comprise the first 3½ years of God's wrath, and it is seven bowl judgments which will conclude the wrath of God and the last 3½ years of the tribulation period which was for seven years.

Vs.1-4: *"Then I saw another sign in heaven, great and marvelous: seven angels having the seven last plagues, for in them the wrath of God is complete. And*

I saw something like a sea of glass mingled with fire, and those who have the victory over the beast, over his image and over his mark and over the number of his name, standing on the sea of glass, having harps of God. They sing the song of Moses, the servant of God, and the song of the Lamb, saying: "Great and marvelous are Your works, Lord God Almighty! Just and true are Your ways, O King of the saints! Who shall not fear You, O Lord, and glorify Your name? For You alone are holy. For all nations shall come and worship before You, for Your judgments have been manifested."

Here John is shown the seven angels who have the seven last plagues which will complete the wrath of God. This clearly shows that the first 3½ years were also the *"wrath of God."* Then John sees the saints whom Jesus reaped from the earth in chapt.14:14-17 and their situation before the throne singing praises and worshipping God. These Tribulation saints sing the song of Moses and the Lamb because they were both delivered from bondage <u>and</u> redeemed to God by the blood of the Lamb. There will be no more battles to be fought, no more temptations to endure, but absolute peace in the glory and majesty of the presence of the Lord. The tribulation saints, like us, will have received their glorified bodies. The victory of the tribulation saints over the beast was not that they defeated him but that by faith they persevered to the end.

Vs.5-8: *"After these things I looked, and behold, the temple of the tabernacle of the testimony in heaven was opened. And out of the temple came the seven angels having the seven plagues, clothed in pure bright linen, and having their chests girded with golden bands. Then one of the four living creatures gave to the seven angels seven golden bowls full of the wrath of God who lives forever and ever. The temple was filled with smoke from the glory of God and from His power, and no one was able to enter the temple till the seven plagues of the seven angels were completed."*

The temple of the tabernacle of testimony in heaven was opened. It is interesting that the word *mar-too'-re-on*, used here for 'testimony,' has the same root word as martyr, *mar-toss*. As we mentioned earlier, this tabernacle is not to be confused with the one which Moses built. That tabernacle was merely a copy and shadow of these heavenly things which John is being shown (Hebrews 8:4-5). The phrase, "seven last plagues" seems to indicate that Christ is going to return to earth to establish His kingdom right after these plagues are completed. The apparel of these angels is spectacular. Whether this indicates that they are archangels or even some higher rank we don't know. Notice it is one of the four living creatures that gives the seven angels the seven bowls of God's wrath. This might indicate that the four living creatures are of a higher rank than the angels. Imagine, soon we are going to see them as we presently see one another.

The temple is filled with smoke from the glory of God and from His power, and no one is able to enter the temple till the seven plagues of the seven angels are completed. Until that time, God alone will inhabit His temple. Which makes me think, 'how often do we think about how God feels?' God has feelings. He can grieve. Ps.78:40; 95:10; Isa.63:10 and Jer.5:3 are a few examples of those things which grieve His great heart. We may also discover those things in which God takes delight by reading, Ps.16:3; 147:10; Prov.11:1 & 20; 12:22: 15:8; and Jer.9:24. However, God rejoices too. In Zephaniah 3:17 we are told, *"He will rejoice over you with gladness, He will quiet you with His love, He will rejoice over you with singing."* Revelation 15:8 to me is a sad and sobering scene as if God just wants to be alone as Heaven anticipates the completion of His wrath. *"As I live,' says the Lord God, 'I have no pleasure in the death of the wicked, but that the wicked turn from his way and live. Turn, turn from your evil ways! For why should you die,"* (Ezek 33:11).

CHAPTER 16

THE SEVEN BOWL JUDGMENTS

Revelation 16 has often been called the "great" chapter because we are shown the great city, the great river is dried up, there is the great earthquake, and lastly the great hail. To understand the severity of God's judgments we must remember that for around 6,000 years God has exhausted every effort to draw mankind into relationship with Him and to be a participant in His plan and program. And yet the majority of mankind has rejected all God had provided and now in these last days the unbelieving world has persecuted, in the most inhumane way, the last of His children, those who come to faith in Jesus Christ during the last 3½ years. I believe the measure of God's judgment exactly corresponds with the measure of man's rebellion against God. God is just. *"Righteousness and justice are the foundation of Your throne; Mercy and truth go before Your face,"* (Ps 89:14). *"The judgments of the Lord are true and righteous altogether,"* (Ps 19:9).

"Evil men do not understand justice, but those who seek the Lord understand all," (Prov 28:5).

One of the first things we will notice in each of these bowl judgements is that they only effect those who have the mark of the beast on their hand or forehead. Here we have another clear indication that there are people who do get saved after the rapture and after the reaping of chapter 14 and are shielded from this judgment. This distinction was also applied during the plagues in Egypt which were poured out on Pharaoh and his people, but had no effect on the land of Goshen and God's people. As believers, we might experience tribulation and trials in this life, but we will not experience God's wrath being poured out on an unbelieving, rebellious world.

Another thing to note is that as impossible as it is for us to imagine the reality of these judgments there is no reason for us to think that they are merely symbolic.

First Bowl Judgment:

Vs.1-2: *"Then I heard a loud voice from the temple saying to the seven angels, 'Go and pour out the bowls of the wrath of God on the earth.'" So the first went and poured out his bowl upon the earth, and a foul and loathsome sore came upon the men who had the mark of the beast and those who worshiped his image."*

Loathsome sores come upon only those men who have the mark of the beast and who worship his image. In other words there are some who haven't taken the mark or worshiped his image. We must keep in mind that those who <u>have</u> taken the mark of the beast are beyond repentance because they have willing selected allegiance to anti-christ and have been sealed with his mark.

Second Bowl Judgment:

Vs.3: *"Then the second angel poured out his bowl on the sea, and it became blood as of a dead man; and every living creature in the sea died."*

The sea turns to blood and every living creature in the sea dies. This judgment comes upon those who called for the blood of believers to be shed and now they have more blood than they could ever comprehend. At this point, all sea travel, trade and commerce end.

Third Bowl Judgment:

Vs.4-6: *"Then the third angel poured out his bowl on the rivers and springs of water, and they became blood. And I heard the angel of the waters saying:*

"You are righteous, O Lord, the One who is and who was and who is to be, because You have judged these things. For they have shed the blood of saints

and prophets, and You have given them blood to drink. For it is their just due."

All the rivers and springs of water become blood and the angel of the waters announces the righteousness of God's judgment adding, *"They have shed the blood of the saints and the prophets, and you have given them blood to drink. For it is their just due."* All *fresh* water becomes blood.

Vs.7 : *"And I heard another from the altar saying, "Even so, Lord God Almighty, true and righteous are Your judgments."*

Yet another angel declares the truth and righteousness of God's judgments, echoing the proclamation of a much earlier time found in Deuteronomy 32:3-4, *"For I proclaim the name of the Lord: Ascribe greatness to our God. He is the Rock, His work is perfect; For all His ways are justice, a God of truth and without injustice; Righteous and upright is He."* Amen.

Fourth Bowl Judgment:

Vs.8-9: *"Then the fourth angel poured out his bowl on the sun, and power was given to him to scorch men with fire. And men were scorched with great heat, and they blasphemed the name of God who has power over these plagues; and they did not repent and give Him glory."*

The sun scorches men with fire. Men's response is

not to repent and give God glory but rather to blaspheme the name of God. It would appear that after rejecting the love of God repeatedly and deliberately people come to a point where their hearts become caurterized. (Rom.1:28 and 2 Tim. 4:1-2).

The Fifth Bowl Judgment:

Vs.10-11: *"Then the fifth angel poured out his bowl on the throne of the beast, and his kingdom became full of darkness; and they gnawed their tongues because of the pain. They blasphemed the God of heaven because of their pains and their sores, and did not repent of their deeds."*

The beast and his kingdom are the object of this judgment. His kingdom becomes filled with a darkness that can be felt and which is actually so painful that men gnaw their tongues because of the pain of this oppressive darkness and of the sores. Again, the response of unrepentant men is to blaspheme the God of Heaven who has offered forgiveness and cleansing for multiple millennia. Here we have a terrifying example of just how hard men's hearts can become if they do not repent. Likewise many today who refuse to hear the voice of God will have their personal kingdom plunged into darkness. How hard a person's heart must be to walk in darkness when light is so close and readily accessible. Read Jer.13:16.

The Sixth Bowl Judgment:

Vs.12-14: *"Then the sixth angel poured out his bowl on the great river Euphrates, and its water was dried up, so that the way of the kings from the east might be prepared. And I saw three unclean spirits like frogs coming out of the mouth of the dragon, out of the mouth of the beast, and out of the mouth of the false prophet. For they are spirits of demons, performing signs, which go out to the kings of the earth and of the whole world, to gather them to the battle of that great day of God Almighty."*

The sixth bowl judgement is the drying up of the waters of the great river Euphrates to make way for all the kings of the east to join in that great battle of Armageddon. In understanding Scripture, context is key therefore, we recognize that these "kings of the east" do not refer to China because we are plainly told they are, *"the kings of the earth and of the whole world."* In addition, three unclean spirits, like frogs, come out of the mouths of the *dragon,* the *beast,* and the *false prophet*: the unholy trinity. This unholy alliance uses "lying signs and wonders" (2 Thess.2:9) which influence every world leader to gather to fight against God <u>on that great day of God Almighty</u>. This powerful spiritual deception is literal but not material, but are actual spirits of demons. Take note, we are not being told that this battle is fought at this point in time, but simply that the armies begin to move to the place where the battle will be fought: Armageddon, also called the valley of Megido.

Vs.15-16: *"Behold, I am coming as a thief. Blessed is he who watches, and keeps his garments, lest he walk naked and they see his shame." And they gathered them together to the place called in Hebrew, Armageddon."*

In verse fifteen Jesus declares His soon return and repeats the admonition to all believers to keep watch. In other words, to stay awake. We must always remember that at no point in time can we hope to establish our own righteousness by our own good works. To do so results in being found naked and ashamed.

Read Rom. 4:5, 10:3; Phil. 3:9; 2 Cor.5:3 and Rom.3:21,22, and Isa.61:10.

Considering all the devastation which has taken place at this point we can only imagine how long it would take for all the armies of the whole world to be assembled in one location. In any case, the armies of earth are gathering for the battle of Armageddon. We will be told about the actual battle in chapter 19:19.

The Seventh Bowl Judgment:

Vs.17-21: *"Then the seventh angel poured out his bowl into the air, and a loud voice came out of the temple of heaven, from the throne, saying, 'It is done!'*

And there were noises and thunderings and lightnings; and there was a great earthquake, such a mighty and great earthquake as had not occurred since men were on the earth. Now the great city was divided into three parts, and the cities of the nations fell."

It is interesting to note that Satan is called the prince of the power of the air (Ephesians 2:2), and this bowl judgment is poured out on the air and is therefore a direct judgment upon the entire sphere of Satan's power and influence. At this point Satan has lost all dominion and power. If we recall 15:8 we understand that the loud voice is God's because He is the only one in the temple at this point, and only Almighty God can make such a declaration because, after all, it is "the wrath of God" that is being completed. When the last bowl judgment is poured out God's wrath is complete. All of God's judgments are righteous because everyone on earth had the same opportunity to receive Jesus Christ as their Lord and Savior. If the opportunity to repent was not offered to all then God's judgment would be unrighteous.

Everything is made flat: mountains sink, buildings and houses fall. The noises and the earthquake are a result of the seventh bowl being poured into the air. Consider there is destruction from above and below. Keep in mind that at this point all believing Jews are safely tucked away in the wilderness. It is easy, when we look at prophecies that occur after the rapture to think that it has nothing to do with us. But that is not true, God pronounced a special blessing on those who read or hear the prophecies of this great book and *"keep those things which are written in it,"*(Rev.1:3 and 22:18) for a reason. He says, *"for the time is near,"* (Rev.220). We live in a vile world and are subject to ceaseless temptations every day. We would be wise to heed the warnings which are given to the Tribulation saints as we see the time of the Rapture drawing nearer. As Jesus said, *"Now when these things <u>begin</u> to happen, look up and lift up your heads, because your redemption draws near". . . "Watch therefore, and pray always that you may be counted worthy to escape all these things that will come to pass, and to stand before the Son of Man". "And do this, <u>knowing the time</u>, that now it is high time to awake out of sleep; for now our salvation is nearer than when we first believed,"* (Luke 21:28 emphasis added & 36 and Rom 13:11-12 emphasis added).

Vs.19-21: *"And great Babylon was remembered before God, to give her the cup of the wine of the fierceness of His wrath. Then every island fled away, and the mountains were not found. And great hail from heaven fell upon men, each hailstone about the weight of a talent. Men blasphemed God because of the plague of the hail, since that plague was exceedingly great."*

This great earthquake causes the great city to be divided into three parts, and all the cities of all the nations will fall to the ground. The destruction which is prophesied for Babylon is severe, not only a mere division into three parts, but an overwhelming devastation resulting in her complete unfitness for further habitation. Now God is going to deal directly with the world system which has been united by a one-world religion. Babylon is not only a *place,* but symbolizes the essence of thought, purpose, and identity that is vehemently opposed to God's name, to His glory, and to His purposes. This is why believers are exhorted to, *"Not be conformed to this world, but be transformed by the renewing of your mind, that you may prove what is that good and acceptable and perfect will of God,"* (Rom 12:2 also James 4:4 and 1 Jn2:15-17). The designation, "Babylon" as used in the book of Revelation signifies not only where pagan religion and the present world system had its birth, but also signifies all that is perverse. God will not be mocked; His judgement will fall on those who have followed Satan and his adulterous ways, and they will receive the full measure of God's wrath.

CHAPTER 17

MYSTERY BABYLON THE GREAT; THE SCARLET WOMEN SITTING ON THE SCARLET BEAST

Rev 17:1-6: *"Then one of the seven angels who had the seven bowls came and talked with me, saying to me, "Come, I will show you the judgment of the great harlot who sits on many waters, with whom the kings of the earth committed fornication, and the inhabitants of the earth were made drunk with the wine of her fornication. So he carried me away in the Spirit into the wilderness. And I saw a woman sitting on a scarlet beast which was full of names of blasphemy, having seven heads and ten horns. The woman was arrayed in purple and scarlet, and adorned with gold and precious stones and pearls, having in her hand a golden cup full of abominations and the filthiness of her fornication. And on her forehead a name was written: MYSTERY, BABYLON THE GREAT, THE MOTHER OF HARLOTS AND OF*

THE ABOMINATIONS OF THE EARTH. I saw the woman, drunk with the blood of the saints and with the blood of the martyrs of Jesus. And when I saw her, I marveled with great amazement."

In this chapter we will be given a thorough understanding of *Babylon* which is not only given the title "Mystery Babylon The Great", but also the title, "Mother". We will discover that Babylon is not merely a region or a city. Rather, Babylon is in concept the very essence of everything that has opposed God and His purposes from the beginning, and also that which gave birth to everything that is unfaithful to God and all that is an abomination in His sight. This 'woman' who sits atop the beast is a metaphor for the great city, possibly Rome, or religious Babylon, and the beast is carrying her (v.7). In vs.18 the angel reveals to John the identity of the woman. She is *"that great city which reigns over the kings of the earth."* We already know the identity of the beast as anti-Christ operating in all of Satan's power. Notice the beast is scarlet and the woman is arrayed in purple and scarlet, colors which depict wealth and power. Take note of the number of references to Babylon in Revelation: 14:8; 16:19; and 17:5. As corrupt and powerful as Babylon has been throughout history she will come to a quick, and violent end. Ultimately evil will not go unpunished.

A Brief History of Babylon: We recall that the first world religion was established in an actual region of the world called Shinar (Southern Mesopotamia). This is the region where Nimrod began his kingdom called Babel (Gen. 10.10). In Gen.10:19 we are informed that Nimrod, which possibly means "Let Us Revolt", was "a mighty hunter before the Lord" ("against" the Lord: Jewish Encyclopedia). He was not a hunter of animals, but of men: a conqueror. We find out about the first one-world religion that Nimrod attempted to establish in Genesis 11:4-9. I find it interesting to note that the empire of Babylon was always an enemy of Israel. Israel was eventually taken into captivity at the time when King Nebuchadnezzar ruled Babylon, and Babylon was the head of gold in the King's dream. Read Daniel 2:31-45

Vs.1-6: *"Then one of the seven angels who had the seven bowls came and talked with me, saying to me, "Come, I will show you the judgment of the great harlot who sits on many waters, with whom the kings of the earth committed fornication, and the inhabitants of the earth were made drunk with the wine of her fornication." So he carried me away in the Spirit into the wilderness. And I saw a woman sitting on a scarlet beast which was full of names of blasphemy, having seven heads and ten horns. The woman was arrayed in purple and scarlet, and adorned with gold and precious stones and pearls, having in her hand a golden cup full of abominations and the filthiness of her fornication. And on her forehead a name was written: MYSTERY, BABYLON THE GREAT, THE MOTHER OF HARLOTS AND OF THE ABOMINATIONS OF THE EARTH. I saw the woman, drunk with the blood of the saints and with the blood of the martyrs of Jesus. And when I saw her, I marveled with great amazement.*"

John is invited by the angel to witness the judgment of the great harlot, the world religious system. The woman has written on her forehead the name 'Mystery Bablyon The Great, The Mother Of Harlots And Of The Abominations Of The Earth,' because while having promoted herself as being faithful to God she had in fact played the harlot with the governments of the world and its many false religions. Now the "mystery" regarding Babylon is unveiled for us, namely that each of these facets of life: politics, economics, social trends, and religion, have always been tightly intertwined. Not one facet operates apart from the other. The inhabitants of earth have been seduced and have become intoxicated with the appeal of all that Mystery Babylon has to offer, and she touches every aspect of life. There is not one person, people group, or nation which is not influenced by this great harlot and the vast scope of her reach.

Vs.7-8: *"But the angel said to me, "Why did you marvel? I will tell you the mystery of the woman and of the beast that carries her, which has the seven heads and the ten horns. The beast that you saw was, and is not, and will ascend out of the bottomless pit (likely the same one who killed the two witnesses) and go to perdition. And those who dwell on the earth will marvel, whose names are not written in the Book of Life from the foundation of the world, when they see the beast that was, and is not, and yet is."*

For now, all of the unsaved world is absolutely enamored with and utterly deceived by the beast. They do not worship the beast because things are so great but because they are convinced it is the only chance of defeating Christ, the Lamb who is unleashing these judgements!

Vs.9-11: *"Here is the mind which has wisdom: The seven heads are seven mountains on which the woman sits. There are also seven kings. Five have fallen, one is, and the other has not yet come. And when he comes, he must continue a short time. The beast that was, and is not, is himself also the eighth, and is of the seven, and is going to perdition."*

Many respectable Bible teachers have associated the "seven mountains" with the city of Rome because Rome sits on seven hills. However, we are plainly told here that the <u>seven heads</u> are the seven mountains on which the woman sits. I believe this is simply repetition for the sake of emphasis. We recall from 13:1 that the beast which rises out of the sea has <u>seven heads</u> and here John sees the woman "sitting on a beast which has names full of blasphemy," which is the same description of the beast out of the sea. This is why I believe that the *seven heads/seven mountains* refers to <u>seats of power</u>, rather than literal mountains. I have very little comment to make on this portion because it is not the focus of the contribution I hope to make to understanding Revelation. We know from the account of the ten horns that ten nations or regions will come into power over the whole earth but will then give all their power and authority to the anti-Christ. This is very intriguing, however, I believe the specifics cannot be known until the Tribulation has actually commenced and therefore it is pointless to speculate.

Vs. 12-18: *"The ten horns which you saw are ten kings who have received no kingdom as yet, but they receive authority for one hour as kings with the beast. These are of one mind, and they will give their power and authority to the beast. These will make war with the Lamb, and the Lamb will overcome them, for He is Lord of lords and King of kings; and those who are with Him are called, chosen, and faithful. Then he said to me, "The waters which you saw, where the harlot sits, are peoples, multitudes, nations, and tongues.*

And the ten horns which you saw on the beast, these will hate the harlot, make her desolate and naked, eat her flesh and burn her with fire. For God has put it into their hearts to fulfill His purpose, to be of one mind, and to give their kingdom to the beast, until the words of God are fulfilled. And the woman whom you saw is that great city which reigns over the kings of the earth."

We read in Vs. 1 that this woman "sits on many waters" which in v.15 the angel discloses to John are "peoples, multitudes, nations, and tongues." In this portion we see that all who have taken the mark and follow the beast will become very fundamental in their faith and follow the beast alone, hating the religious system of Babylon that has controlled the world. Whereas the beast refers to political and economic Babylon, the woman sitting on that beast is a religious system, and thus her title mystery, Babylon the great, etc. Governments and kingdom have come and gone each being in essence, *Babylon*. However, the <u>religious</u> aspect of Babylon while perhaps changing in appearance from time to time has yet remained the harlot for multiple millenia. Throughout history Satan has used religion to control the masses and hinder people from coming to God. Today there are more religious systems than we have time to write about, but in the end they will morph into one system that will have the anti-Christ as the object of their worship.

In vs.18 the angel informs John that the woman's identity is *"that great city which reigns over the kings of the earth."* So let us consider, is there any city that has held such immense influence over the nations and to such an extent that could be described as actually having *reigned over the kings of the earth?* Yes, there has been one city of which that could be said and that city is Rome. All religious systems are based on so-called mystery knowledge, rules, ceremonies, and doctrines which are outside of scripture. Whereas, true faith in Jesus Christ is simple, open, pure, and holy. Jesus said, *"Assuredly, I say to you, whoever does not receive the kingdom of God as a little child will by no means enter it,"* (Luke 18:17). Religion on the other hand, is based on secrets, power, and corruption. An example is the Roman Catholic Church. The Roman church is called *she*, her colors are scarlet and purple. The gold, pearls, and precious stones which she is bedecked with can be plainly seen at a typical event held at St. Peter's Basilica in Rome, Italy. The altar is laden with ornaments, and the golden cup can be seen in the hands of the pope each time he conducts the mass. History documents that she has surely drunk the blood of the saints and martyrs. During the 300 years of the Roman Catholic Inquisition, Rome put to death an estimated 36,000,000 people. In any case, God sees this woman as filthy and disgusting, drunk with the blood of the saints and the martyrs of Jesus Christ.

John is amazed to vividly see this world religious system which identifies herself as the church, clothed in the finest apparel and possessing the most costly objects but which in reality is filthy, disgusting, and drunk with the blood of saints.

This religious system is drunk on the blood of the <u>saints</u> and the <u>martyrs</u> specifically talking about <u>believers in Jesus Christ</u>, not those who have been killed for the sake of their *religion*. Many religions murder and brutalize those within their own ranks. This portion however is in reference to the fact that <u>religious systems</u> will never tolerate those who hold to the simple truth of faith in the Person of Jesus Christ and His atoning and redemptive work, but will instead destroy those who hold to that faith. The book of Acts as well as "Fox's Book Of Martyrs" well document this fact. Right now in our nation if you claim to believe in God as the Creator of all things you are looked upon with distain. Before the Lord called me into the ministry I was a high school science teacher, and for the past seven years I have been a substitute teacher in our local high school. I can tell you from experience that the argument for the defense in the famous Scopes trial, which took place less than 100 years ago, that the theory of Evolution should be allowed to be taught in public school, is now completely denied to Creationists. It is now unlawful to teach Creation in public school.

Generally speaking, most all religious systems

come to a point where the adherents eventually tend to worship the religious system more than the god of that system. We know that Satan's fall was the result of his seeking to exalt himself above Almighty God. Therefore, he and his anti-Christ will not tolerate worship being diverted from them to any religious system. This is the reason why the woman/religious system will be devoured by the beast.

CHAPTER 18

THE FALL OF BABYLON

Revelation 18:1-3: *"After these things I saw another angel coming down from heaven, having great authority, and the earth was illuminated with his glory. And he cried mightily with a loud voice, saying, "Babylon the great is fallen, is fallen, and has become a dwelling place of demons, a prison for every foul spirit, and a cage for every unclean and hated bird! For all the nations have drunk of the wine of the wrath of her fornication, the kings of the earth have committed fornication with her, and the merchants of the earth have become rich through the abundance of her luxury."*

The angel in verse one who announces the fall of Babylon has great authority and is so glorious that the earth is illuminated by him, and we are reminded of the angel mentioned in chapter 10:1 who also was glorious in appearance. Here we see that the designation of "Babylon" refers to all of the world's ethnic groups, political nation states, and the economic systems. There is no segment or aspect of the world that has not been entirely engaged with Babylon.

The entire operation of the world is one big prison system and a trap. Outwardly what the world offers appears luxurious and sophisticated but God sees it as filthy and foul. All too often we read about those who have virtually sold their soul for fame and fortune only to be exploited and then cast aside when their usefulness is finished, left in the prison and cage of the world's lie.

Vs.4-8: *"And I heard another voice from heaven saying, "Come out of her, my people, lest you share in her sins, and lest you receive of her plagues. For her sins have reached to heaven, and God has remembered her iniquities. Render to her just as she rendered to you, and repay her double according to her works; in the cup which she has mixed, mix double for her. In the measure that she glorified herself and lived luxuriously, in the same measure give her torment and sorrow; for she says in her heart, 'I sit as queen, and am no widow, and will not see sorrow.' Therefore her plagues will come in one day — death and mourning and famine. And she will be utterly burned with fire, for strong is the Lord God who judges her."*

Just as the angels which were sent to Sodom and Gomorrah had as their first task to rescue as many as they could out of those cities before they were to be destroyed, so we see here another warning to mankind to, "come out <u>my people</u>." A similar call to separate ourselves from this world system of purpose and thought, as well as from this world's many religions is given to believers in the second letter to the church at Corinth, "*Do not be unequally yoked together with unbelievers. For what fellowship has righteousness with lawlessness? And what communion has light with darkness? And what accord has Christ with Belial? Or what part has a believer with an unbeliever? And what agreement has the temple of God with idols? For you are the temple of the living God. As God has said: "I will dwell in them and walk among them. I will be their God, and they shall be My people." Therefore "Come out from among them and be separate, says the Lord. Do not touch what is unclean, and I will receive you." 'I will be a Father to you, and you shall be My sons and daughters, says the Lord Almighty,*"(2 Cor 6:14-18). Even as believers we can become entangled in all of this world's affairs. Therefore, we must be alert as our enemy indeed roams about as a roaring lion. Even though we will not be here when all this comes upon the world yet this warning applies to all believers now to guard ourselves from the many entrapments of this world. We remember the admonition, "*And do this, knowing the time, that now it is high time to awake out of sleep; for now our salvation is nearer than when we first believed,*" (Rom 13:11).

Vs.9-13: *"The kings of the earth who committed fornication and lived luxuriously with her will weep and lament for her, when they see the smoke of her burning, standing at a distance for fear of her torment, saying, 'Alas, alas, that great city Babylon, that mighty city! For in one hour your judgment has come.' "And the merchants of the earth will weep and mourn over her, for no one buys their merchandise anymore: merchandise of gold and silver, precious stones and pearls, fine linen and purple, silk and scarlet, every kind of citron wood, every kind of object of ivory, every kind of object of most precious wood, bronze, iron, and marble; and cinnamon and incense, fragrant oil and frankincense, wine and oil, fine flour and wheat, cattle and sheep, horses and chariots, and bodies and souls of men."*

The express intent for which the people in Nimrod's time desired to build a city for themselves (Gen.11:4) was specifically to defy the known will of Almighty God. The very purpose of their plan was to be entirely independent of God and contrary to Him. Fast forward to the present world system and we see that every detail whether it be economic, social, political, or religious had its commencement in Gen. 11:4 and has never ceased to operate from that time to the present. However chapter 18 reveals to us the ultimate end of that ages long endeavor which God views as fornication and adultery. The most powerful, most elite, most wealthy of the world now weep and lament as they witness the entire scope of their enterprise come to an utter and complete end in one hour. It is very sobering and chilling to consider that the dealings of the world system hasn't only been in commodities of material things which has enriched them beyond calculation, but in the actual bodies and souls of men. I believe this detail is included because the corrupt world system holds nothing sacred where money is to be made or power is to be advanced. How many innocent people who unwittingly found themselves in the wrong place at the wrong time, who saw something they were never supposed to see and were murdered to protect those involved? Consider the vast magnitude of world-wide human trafficking as well as the abortion industry where money is made at the expense of the most innocent. This has been the dark business of Babylon for multiple millennia. God's judgment is both righteous and just and the blood of the innocent will finally be avenged.

Vs.14-19: *"The fruit that your soul longed for has gone from you, and all the things which are rich and splendid have gone from you, and you shall find them no more at all. The merchants of these things, who became rich by her, will stand at a distance for fear of her torment, weeping and wailing, and saying, 'Alas, alas, that great city that was clothed in fine* linen, purple, and scarlet, and adorned with gold and precious stones and pearls! For in one hour such great riches came to nothing.' Every shipmaster, all who travel by ship, sailors, and as many as trade on the sea, stood at a distance and cried out when they saw the smoke of her burning, saying, 'What is like this great city?' "They threw dust on their heads and cried out, weeping and wailing, and saying, 'Alas, alas, that great city, in which all who had ships on the sea became rich by her wealth! For in one hour she is made desolate."*

Here we observe the world's horrifying realization of the complete and utter loss of their entire investment. That which they sought after was sadly to the peril of their souls as we are warned in 1 Tim 6:9-10, "*But those who desire to be rich fall into temptation and a snare, and into many foolish and harmful lusts which drown men in destruction and perdition. For the love of money is a root of all kinds of evil, for which some have strayed from the faith in their greediness, and pierced themselves through with many sorrows.*" Read also James 5:2. That which they thought would satisfy the longing hunger of their soul is now utterly gone from them, and they shall find them no more at all. The scriptural record of the inventory of the loss leaves no category unaccounted for. But long ago the prophet Isaiah wrote by inspiration of the Holy Spirit, "*Why do you spend money for what is not bread, and your wages for what does not satisfy? Listen carefully to Me, and eat what is good, and let your soul delight itself in abundance. Incline your ear, and come to Me. Hear, and your soul shall live,"* (Isa 55:2-3).

Vs.20-24: *"Rejoice over her, O heaven, and you holy apostles and prophets, for God has avenged you on her"! "Then a mighty angel took up a stone like a great millstone and threw it into the sea, saying, 'Thus with violence the great city Babylon shall be thrown down, and shall not be found anymore. The sound of harpists, musicians, flutists, and trumpeters shall not be heard in you anymore. No craftsman of any craft shall be found in you anymore, and the sound of a millstone shall not be heard in you anymore. The light of a lamp shall not shine in you anymore, and the voice of bridegroom and bride shall not be heard in you anymore. For your merchants were the great men of the earth, for by your sorcery all the nations were deceived. And in her was found the blood of prophets and saints, and of all who were slain on the earth."*

Here we read additional details regarding Babylon's destruction. More importantly we understand that everything which Babylon produced was corrupt not only because it was the means by which all the nations were deceived, but also because it was the incentive for the death of the prophets, saints, and of all who were slain on the earth. The blood of the apostles and prophets is now avenged and so heaven rejoices.

Verses 9-24 describe not only the utter destruction of commercial, social, and political Babylon but of religious Babylon as well. What is truly astonishing is the vast wealth of the Roman Catholic religious system whose seat is in Rome. The wealth of the Vatican is nearly incalculable. In, <u>The Vatican Billions</u>, by Avro Manhattan he sites, "The Vatican's treasure of solid gold has been estimated by the United Nations World Magazine to amount to several billion dollars. A large bulk of this is stored in gold ingots with the U.S. Federal Reserve Bank, while banks in England and Switzerland hold the rest. But this is just a small portion of the wealth of the Vatican, which in the U.S. alone, is greater than that of the five wealthiest giant corporations of the country. When to that is added all the real estate, property, stocks and shares abroad, then the staggering accumulation of the wealth of the Catholic church becomes so formidable as to defy any rational assessment."

Just a cursory examination of the wealth and holdings of the Roman Church staggars the imagination. The power with which the Vatican Bank operates over other banks is nothing short of chilling, and when set alongside of Pope Francis' recent denunciation of wealth one is quite amazed at what is either mind boggling hypocrisy, or sheer blindness. When Mystery Babylon is destroyed the entire world which has worshiped money, wealth, and power will certainly wail and mourn. "*Come now, you rich, weep and howl for your miseries that are coming upon you! Your riches are corrupted, and your garments are moth-eaten. Your gold and silver are corroded, and their corrosion will be a witness against you and will eat your flesh like fire. You have heaped up treasure in the last days. Indeed the wages of the laborers who mowed your fields, which you kept back by fraud, cry out; and the cries of the reapers have reached the ears of the Lord of Sabaoth. You have lived on the earth in pleasure and luxury; you have fattened your hearts as in a day of slaughter. You have condemned, you have murdered the just; he does not resist you,*"(James 5:1-6).

The anti-Christ seemed for a while to be in favor of a religious system that follows a false Christianity, but now shows his true colors because his intention from the beginning was that he be worshiped as god. The world has no grief over the loss of the most powerful religious system ever known which, 'ruled over the kings of the earth,' but rather mourns over the incalculable financial loss.

There will be no rising from the ashes of religious Babylon as social and political Babylon make preparations to make war against the Lamb of God. Money is their god, but money cannot buy their salvation nor can it defeat the God of all creation.

Please understand, it's not a sin to pursue a career, be successful, to have nice possessions, or to be financially secure or affluent. The warning to believers has ever and only been to not <u>trust</u> **in** our possessions, or to lust after wealth and position, or seek to find identity and purpose in that pursuit. The Word of God merely says, *"But those who desire to be rich fall into temptation and a snare, and into many foolish and harmful lusts which drown men in destruction and perdition. For the love of money is a root of all kinds of evil, for which some have strayed from the faith in their greediness, and pierced themselves through with many sorrows,"* (1 Tim 6:9-10).

The entire seven year tribulation period is the wrath of God being poured out on an unbelieving world and so the idea that for the first three and a half years the situation on earth is fairly normal and that it is only during the last three and a half years that world-wide catastrophic and devastating situations begin is not supported by the record of Revelation.

CHAPTER 19

Marriage Supper of The Lamb
The Second Coming of Christ
The Battle Of Armageddon

Vs.1-4: *"After these things I heard a loud voice of a great multitude in heaven, saying, "Alleluia! Salvation and glory and honor and power belong to the Lord our God! For true and righteous are His judgments, because He has judged the great harlot who corrupted the earth with her fornication; and He has avenged on her the blood of His servants shed by her." Again they said, "Alleluia! Her smoke rises up forever and ever!" And the twenty-four elders and the four living creatures fell down and worshiped God who sat on the throne, saying, "Amen! Alleluia!"*

The same phrase, "After these things," is used in Rev. 4:1; 7:1, 9; 9:12; 15:5; 18:1 and finally in 20:3. "After these things" is translated from the Greek, *meta tauta* and literally means "the next thing." And so here once again we are reminded of the chronological flow of the book of Revelation, one event following the next, except for a few intermissions such as we find in chapter 12. Here in chapter 19 the prayer request of the souls under the altar in chapter six and verse 9 is answered. The smoke of the destruction of the great harlot who corrupted the earth with adulterous religion will rise forever and ever. It's shocking to many people to discover that God has nothing to do with religion and religion has nothing to do with God. Religion is mankind's attempt to justify himself in defiance of God's provision of His Son Jesus Christ. Religion is Satan's greatest deception and hell's best kept secret. The powerful seduction of religion has kept men from knowing true forgiveness, cleansing, and new life which comes through faith in Christ alone. Jesus made this very clear when He told the religious leaders of his day, *"Then, in the hearing of all the people, He said to His disciples, "Beware of the scribes, who desire to go around in long robes, love greetings in the marketplaces, the best seats in the synagogues, and the best places at feasts, who devour widows' houses, and for a pretense make long prayers. These will receive greater condemnation"* (Luke 20:45-21:1).*"But woe to you, scribes and Pharisees, hypocrites! For you shut up the kingdom of heaven against men; for you neither go in yourselves, nor do you allow those who are entering to go in." "Woe to you, scribes and Pharisees, hypocrites! For you travel land and sea to win one proselyte, and when he is won, you make him twice as much a son of hell as yourselves,"*(Matt 23:13-15). And so it should be very clear to everyone how Jesus views religious systems and religious hierarchy.

Vs.5-10: *"Then a voice came from the throne, saying, "Praise our God, all you His servants and those who fear Him, both small and great!" And I heard, as it were, the voice of a great multitude, as the sound of many waters and as the sound of mighty thunderings, saying, "Alleluia! For the Lord God Omnipotent reigns! Let us be glad and rejoice and give Him glory, for the marriage of the Lamb has come, and His wife has made herself ready." And to her it was granted to be arrayed in fine linen, clean and bright, for the fine linen is the righteous acts of the saints. Then he said to me, "Write: 'Blessed are those who are called to the marriage supper of the Lamb!'" And he said to me, "These are the true sayings of God." And I fell at his feet to worship him. But he said to me, See that you do not do that! I am your fellow servant, and of your brethren who have the testimony of Jesus. Worship God! For the testimony of Jesus is the spirit of prophecy."*

Heaven is thunderous with praise, adoration, and worship to God! The Church is the Bride of Christ (Jn.3:29; 2 Cor.11:2) and a common mistake which many believers make is thinking that the wedding supper of the Lamb takes place in Heaven as soon as the Church is raptured. However, the marriage supper of the Lamb cannot take place until the church is complete and that will not occur until the Tribulation saints have all been gathered in for that great celebration as well. At this point in the record of Revelation that time has now come as the number of their fellow servants, the tribulation saints, has been completed. It would appear that the marriage supper takes place at this point although we are not given any information about it. We will find out more about the Lamb's bride in chapter 21.

Vs.11-16: *"Now I saw heaven opened, and behold, a white horse. And He who sat on him was called Faithful and True, and in righteousness He judges and makes war. His eyes were like a flame of fire, and on His head were many crowns. He had a name written that no one knew except Himself. He was clothed with a robe dipped in blood, and His name is called The Word of God. And the armies in heaven, clothed in fine linen, white and clean, followed Him on white horses. Now out of His mouth goes a sharp sword, that with it He should strike the nations. And He Himself will rule them with a rod of iron. He Himself treads the winepress of the fierceness and wrath of Almighty God. And He has on His robe and on His thigh a name written*: KING OF KINGS AND LORD OF LORDS.*"*

Consider what it means to see heaven opened. It is beyond our ability to fully comprehend what this means because heaven is the dwelling place of God and He is now coming to earth with all the hosts of heaven following Him. *"Thus the Lord my God will come, and all the saints with You,"* (Zech 14:5). The image of a white horse is a warrior going into battle, and this warrior is called Faithful and True. To be faithful means He never forsakes, and True in that no lie can be found in Him. He sees all, knows all, and has the power and authority to judge all mankind. His Name, the name that no one knows but Him, is what constitutes His full identity, something beyond anything we are capable of comprehending.

His robe is dipped in His own blood. The blood stains on His robe are from when He gave His life for us on Calvary. He and no one else is worthy, and it is His blood alone which removes all the guilt and stain of sin from the repentant believer. He is the Word of God to man and for man. How interesting that His robe is dipped in blood and His armies, all believers since creation, are wearing clothing of fine linen, white and clean. It makes perfect sense when we consider that His redemptive blood purifies us of all sin. We, the church, are also His army following Him close behind on white horses.

It's been said many times, 'life is a journey' and I would add, yes it is but it's all about the destination. In other words, life is not about this life – life is all about the life to come. We are going to have real bodies and live in a real place. Our new bodies and our new habitat will be without any sin or corruption. I love the thought that we won't even know how to sin but know only pure worship of the Living God, who alone is worthy of all our praise.

Vs.17-21: *"Then I saw an angel standing in the sun; and he cried with a loud voice, saying to all the birds that fly in the midst of heaven, "Come and gather together for the supper of the great God, that you may eat the flesh of kings, the flesh of captains, the flesh of mighty men, the flesh of horses and of those who sit on them, and the flesh of all people, free and slave, both small and great." And I saw the beast, the kings of the earth, and their armies, gathered together to make war against Him who sat on the horse and against His army. Then the beast was captured, and with him the false prophet who worked signs in his presence, by which he deceived those who received the mark of the beast and those who worshiped his image. These two were cast alive into the lake of fire burning with brimstone. And the rest were killed with the sword which proceeded from the mouth of Him who sat on the horse. And all the birds were filled with their flesh."*

We see the final outcome of the ignorance and arrogance of rebellion against the Almighty God. This is a gruesome scene indeed. *"For judgment is without mercy to the one who has shown no mercy,"* (James

2:13). We recall 2 Peter 3:9, *"He wishes for none to perish, but for all to come to salvation."* God's grace has removed judgment from all those who have called upon the Name of the Lord. *"There is therefore **now** <u>no condemnation to those who are in Christ Jesus</u>, who do not walk according to the flesh, but according to the Spirit. For the law of the Spirit of life in Christ Jesus has made me free from the law of sin and death,"* (Rom 8:1-3 emphasis added).

In contrast, judgment falls on those who refuse His free gift of salvation that comes by His grace alone, not by anything we have done to accomplish it. The choice is clear, our final judgement and our final destination is determined by the one choice we make to either receive or to reject Jesus Christ. Believers are not perfect in performance but through faith in the atoning work of Jesus Christ they are saved from judgment. To choose Christ is to choose life, to reject Christ is to reject life. No one will be in Hell by accident but by their own choice. Death was not part of God's plan and He never intended for man to go to hell. Hell was not created for man but for Satan and his angels (Matt.25:41).

We are then told that the beast is taken, and with him the false prophet that worked false signs and wonders by which he deceived them that had received the mark of the beast and worshipped his image. They both are cast into the lake of fire burning with brimstone.

CHAPTER 20

SATAN IS BOUND
MILLENNIAL REIGN OF CHRIST
GREAT WHITE THRONE OF JUDGMENT

Vs.1-10: *"Then I saw an angel coming down from heaven, having the key to the bottomless pit and a great chain in his hand. He laid hold of the dragon, that serpent of old, who is the Devil and Satan, and bound him for a thousand years; and he cast him into the bottomless pit, and shut him up, and set a seal on him, so that he should deceive the nations no more till the thousand years were finished. But after these things he must be released for a little while. And I saw thrones, and they sat on them, and judgment was committed to them. Then I saw the souls of those who had been beheaded for their witness to Jesus and for the word of God, who had not worshiped the beast or his image, and had not received his mark on their foreheads or on their hands. And they lived and reigned with Christ for a thousand years. But the rest of the dead did not live again until the thousand years were finished. This is the first resurrection. Blessed and holy is he who has part in the first resurrection. Over such the second death has no power, but they shall be priests of God and of Christ, and shall reign with Him a thousand years. Now when the thousand years have expired, Satan will be released from his prison and will go out to deceive the nations which are in the four corners of the earth, Gog and Magog, to gather them together to battle, whose number is as the sand of the sea. They went up on the breadth of the earth and surrounded the camp of the saints and the beloved city. And fire came down from God out of heaven and devoured them. The devil, who deceived them, was cast into the lake of fire and brimstone where the beast and the false prophet are. And they will be tormented day and night forever and ever."*

We remember that Satan was no match for Michael the archangel in chapter 12. I believe it is most likely that this angel is the same angel who was given the key to the bottomless pit in chapter nine when the demon locust army was released. This angel simply grabs Satan with one hand and has the chain to bind him in his other hand. At this point, the devil is utterly exposed for the fraud that he is and his time of rebellion and deception has been suspended for 1,000 years. Satan thought he could ascend above God and now he is brought down to the pit. *"Yet you shall be brought down to Sheol, to the lowest depths of the Pit. Those who see you will gaze at you, and consider you, saying: 'Is this the man who made the earth tremble, who shook kingdoms, who made the world as a wilderness and destroyed its cities, who did not open the house of his prisoners,"* (Isa 14:15-17)?

Satan is bound for a thousand years, and is prohibited from deceiving the nations for that period of time. This tells us several things. First, Satan can only go as far as the Lord allows. Second, at the end of the thousand years Satan will be released and permitted to deceive the nations one last time. Consider that at this point in John's narrative the earth has existed in a state of paradise for one thousand years. Under the perfect and holy rulership of Jesus Christ, world conditions have been perfect. Perfect justice, perfect environment, everything is perfect. Lawlessness is kept in check by the "rod of iron" with which Jesus rules. Rebellion has been subdued but not obliterated. Therefore, mortals born during this perfect age must also be given the opportunity to freely choose to follow King Jesus just as every other person who ever lived had the free will choice. If there are no options, no alternatives, the concept of choice is nullified. Like all of fallen humanity, those born during the Millenniel Kingdom will be subject to all of the temptations of the flesh. Pride, malice, lust, greed, deceitfulness, vanity, etc. are all active and present during the 1,000 year reign of Christ. Therefore, these people must also have an opportunity to choose faith in Christ. God has never forced anyone to obey Him. To me this is one of the most amazing portions of Scripture. How could anyone live through a thousand years of God's perfection and then choose to rebel? Remember, those born during this time had the choice to submit to Jesus' rule or not. Therefore in order to expose those who are not following King Jesus in their hearts, Satan is released and permitted to deceive the nations one last time. Faith in the Lord is always a choice, not a right or a decree. What is so amazing to me is that a vast multitude choose to follow Satan. However, Satan's deception this time around is short lived, and those who are deceived by him face eternal punishment with him. After his defeat Satan joins the anti-Christ and false prophet in the lake of fire where they are tormented day and night forever and ever.

Revelation 21:8 is the answer to those who promote the idea that everyone will eventually wind up in heaven, an idea which is asserted even by some who profess to believe the Bible. This is a deception and will serve to lull souls into a false security regarding salvation. Will someone claim to be more just than God? Can anyone claim to be more loving than God? This is the position of those who deny the plain truth of Rev. 21:8.

It is made clear that we who are part of the church age along with the tribulation saints will have the same privilege of reigning with Christ for a thousand years. This will be an encouragement to the tribulation saints, as they read this portion during the greatest tribulation Christians have ever faced, *"If we endure, we shall also reign with Him,"* (2 Timothy 2:12). In verse 6 we see that it is very clear that both the pre- and post-tribulation saints are considered to have taken part in the first resurrection. The first resurrection began with the resurrection of Christ, continues with the rapture of the church, and will conclude with the tribulation saints who are martyred and then resurrected (or 'reaped') in Revelation 15:2. On the other hand, the second resurrection is that of the unrighteous dead. The second death mentioned in this portion is the lake of fire. We are to see in Revelation 21:8, *"the cowardly, unbelieving, abominable, murderers, sexually immoral, sorcerers, idolaters, and all liars shall have their part in the lake which burns with fire and brimstone, which is the second death."*

Vs.11-15: *"Then I saw a great white throne and Him who sat on it, from whose face the earth and the heaven fled away. And there was found no place for them. And I saw the dead, small and great, standing before God, and books were opened. And another book was opened, which is the Book of Life. And the dead were judged according to their works, by the things which were written in the books. The sea gave up the dead who were in it, and Death and Hades delivered up the dead who were in them. And they were judged, each one according to his works. Then Death and Hades were cast into the lake of fire. This is the second death. And anyone not found written in the Book of Life was cast into the lake of fire."*

Death for the unbeliever is not the end. There is no nirvana, there is no reincarnation, and there is no purgatory. There is to be judgment when every human being who ever lived and who did not receive God's gracious gift of salvation by grace through faith alone will stand before God all by themselves and give an account for their life. By these verses we understand that the souls of every unbeliever who has ever died has been held in Hades, and their souls will meet their resurrected bodies to now face judgment. The Book of Life is opened just to show those who are now facing judgment that their name is not written in it.

For the believer and unbeliever alike, who you are as an individual person, is not a body - you merely possess a body as a vehicle of animation and expression. However, your soul which is the essence of who you are, your personality and your identity as a singular individual, is not material it is spiritual. After physical death the eternal soul of a believer goes directly to be consciously aware of who they are in the presence of Jesus forever and ever and the eternal soul of the unbeliever goes directly to hell and eventually to the Lake of Fire forever and ever.

CHAPTER 21

New Heaven and New Earth
The New Jerusalem

Both of chapters twenty-one and twenty-two are the glorious culmination of God's plan of salvation, which He purposed before the foundation of the earth (1Pet.1:20; Rev.13:8). Talk about a bright future! We read in Jer.29:11, *"For I know the thoughts that I think toward you, says the Lord, thoughts of peace and not of evil, to give you a future and a hope,"* which is ultimately fulfilled in the New Jerusalem and the river of life that flows through it. Consider all that the believer has to look forward to: the rapture, the return with Jesus, His millennial reign, ruling with Him, then if that were not enough, the new heaven and earth.

Rev 21:1-8: *"Now I saw a new heaven and a new earth, for the first heaven and the first earth had passed away. Also there was no more sea. Then I, John, saw the holy city, New Jerusalem, coming down out of heaven from God, prepared as a bride adorned for her husband. And I heard a loud voice from heaven saying, "Behold, the tabernacle of God is with men, and He will dwell with them, and they shall be His people. God Himself will be with them and be their God. And God will wipe away every tear from their eyes; there shall be no more death, nor sorrow, nor crying. There shall be no more pain, for the former things have passed away." Then He who sat on the throne said, "Behold, I make all things new." And He said to me, "Write, for these words are true and faithful." And He said to me, "It is done! I am the Alpha and the Omega, the Beginning and the End. I will give of the fountain of the water of life freely to him who thirsts. He who overcomes shall inherit all things, and I will be his God and he shall be My son. But the cowardly, unbelieving, abominable, murderers, sexually immoral, sorcerers, idolaters, and all liars shall have their part in the lake which burns with fire and brimstone, which is the second death."*

Remember in vs.11 we were informed that heaven and earth fled away from the face of Him who sat on the white throne, and now John is shown a new heaven and a new earth. Like a number of other concepts which have been revealed in the book of Revelation which we cannot fully grasp, likewise how the Church is to be the Bride of Christ *and* the New Jerusalem is a mystery that will be fully understood at that time. What we do grasp is that God's purpose from the beginning was to dwell, or *tabernacle*, with mankind. Now it is done. God's people have been perfected and now He can dwell with them. His direct presence will be perpetual. The wonderful promise that, *"he who overcomes shall inherit all things, and I will be his God and he shall be My son,"* (Rev.21:7) will be realized by all those who have put their faith in Jesus Christ and have been born again of the Spirit (John 3:3-8). Although we stumble and fall and we struggle and fail, still we continue to run to Jesus and *confess our sins* (1Jn.1:9), and we *continue in the faith* (Col. 1:23). *"For whatever is born of God overcomes the world. And this is the victory that has overcome the world — our faith. Who is he who overcomes the world, but he who believes that Jesus is the Son of God,"* (1 John 5:4-5). All our hope and confidence is in Jesus. He who promised is faithful. *"Blessed be the God and Father of our Lord Jesus Christ, who according to His abundant mercy has begotten us again to a living hope through the resurrection of Jesus Christ from the dead, to an inheritance incorruptible and undefiled and that does not fade away, reserved in heaven for you, who are kept by the power of God through faith for salvation ready to be revealed in the last time,"* (1 Peter 1:3-5 emphasis added). Praise Jesus. All things are made new, an entirely new order of existence on every level for humanity and the universe. Never again for all eternity will there be intrusion of anything that is other than God's perfect and holy will and order, and which brings glory to His great name.

Vs.9-21: *"Then one of the seven angels who had the seven bowls filled with the seven last plagues came to me and talked with me, saying, "Come, I will show you the bride, the Lamb's wife." And he carried me away in the Spirit to a great and high mountain, and showed me the great city, the holy Jerusalem, descending out of heaven from God, having the glory of God. Her light was like a most precious stone, like a jasper stone, clear as crystal. Also she had a great and high wall with twelve gates, and twelve angels at the gates, and names written on them, which are the names of the twelve tribes of the children of Israel: three gates on the east, three gates on the north, three gates on the south, and three gates on the west. Now the wall of the city had twelve foundations, and on them were the names of the twelve apostles of the Lamb. And he who talked with me had a gold reed to measure the city, its gates, and its wall. The city is laid out as a square; its length is as great as its breadth. And he measured the city with the reed: twelve thousand furlongs. Its length, breadth, and height are equal. Then he measured its wall: one hundred and forty-four cubits, according to the measure of a man, that is, of an angel. The construction of its wall was of jasper; and the city was pure gold, like clear glass. The foundations of the wall of the city were adorned with all kinds of precious stones: the first foundation was jasper, the second sapphire, the third chalcedony, the fourth emerald, the fifth sardonyx, the sixth sardius, the seventh chrysolite, the eighth beryl, the ninth topaz, the tenth chrysoprase, the eleventh jacinth, and the twelfth amethyst. The twelve gates were twelve pearls: each individual gate was of one pearl. And the street of the city was pure gold, like transparent glass."*

Because there is no more sun or moon it would appear that the glory of God is what lights the New Jerusalem. The wall around the city has twelve gates with the names of the twelve tribes written on them, and an angel sits at each of the gates. Consider that the nation of Israel was the agent through which God interfaced with man: Abraham is the father of the nation Israel and God told him that all the nations would be blessed through him (Gen.12:2,3; 18:8); Israel was called to be God's witnesses (Isa. 43:10,12; 44:8); Jesus Christ, God incarnate, was of the tribe of Judah (Jn.1:14; Heb.1:1-3; And it was Jews who were the first Church members and to whom God gave the commission to spread His Word (Rom.3:2).

The wall of the city has twelve foundations with the names of the twelve apostles. We remember that is was the twelve apostles who laid the foundation of the gospel of Jesus Christ (1Cor.3:11,12), and each of the foundations is adorned with precious jewels. It's very interesting that the twelve apostles were Jews and the gem-stones mentioned in the wall of the city are the same stones which represented each of the twelve tribes in the ephod of the High Priest. The stones are not listed in the same order as they were on the ephod and I am not sure why the order is different, but perhaps it has something to do with the faithfulness with which each tribe of Israel served God. Again, this whole concept is an eternal one which has been in the mind of God before the foundation of the world, and we are finite creatures. Even though we cannot grasp the eternal concepts and order of things which God will bring about following the Millennial Kingdom yet He has revealed to us as much as we can understand. As we are instructed in 1 Cor 13:12,

"For now we see in a mirror, dimly, but then face to face. Now I know in part, but then I shall know just as I also am known".

However we are specifically informed that the New Jerusalem's length is as great as its breadth, each being twelve thousand furlongs. One furlong is equal to one eighth of a mile. This huge and beautiful city is our future dwelling place. In Hebrews 11:8-16 we are instructed that Abraham "went out" by faith because he was looking for a city whose builder and maker is God. We also are looking for the *"City of the living God, the heavenly Jerusalem, to an innumerable company of angels, to the general assembly and church of the firstborn who are registered in heaven, to God the*

Judge of all, to the spirits of just men made perfect, to Jesus the Mediator of the new covenant, and to the blood of sprinkling that speaks better things than that of Abel," (Heb 12:22-24). (Also read Hebrews13:14). Remember, it's all about the destination.

The wall of the city's height of 216 feet I believe is symbolic of nothing unclean being able to enter, but no doubt there is much more meaning to the height of the wall than just that. The majesty of the city is beyond comprehension. Each gate is a single pearl and the streets are pure gold, like transparent glass. The more pure gold becomes the more transparent it also becomes. We are coming to the end of this great book, and like the ending of any book, final conclusions are made. As Solomon's conclusion was, *"Let us hear the conclusion of the whole matter: Fear God and keep His commandments, for this is man's all. For God will bring every work into judgment, including every secret thing, whether good or evil,"* (Ecclesiastes 12:13-14). How profound and useful is that conclusion for all believers of all time. In the same way, we will find the conclusion of this great Revelation to be just as instructive.

CHAPTER 22

THE RIVER OF LIFE
THE WARNING
JESUS TESTIFIES TO THE CHURCH

Vs.1-5: *"And he showed me a pure river of water of life, clear as crystal, proceeding from the throne of God and of the Lamb. In the middle of its street, and on either side of the river, was the tree of life, which bore twelve fruits, each tree yielding its fruit every month. The leaves of the tree were for the healing of the nations. And there shall be no more curse, but the throne of God and of the Lamb shall be in it, and His servants shall serve Him. They shall see His face, and His name shall be on their foreheads. There shall be no night there: They need no lamp nor light of the sun, for the Lord God gives them light. And they shall reign forever and ever."*

In this present order water is essential for life, our bodies are 70% water. Every living thing requires a daily supply of water. We can go 30-40 days without food, but only two - three days without water. *"Jesus answered and said to her, "Whoever drinks of this water will thirst again, but whoever drinks of the water that I shall give him will never thirst. But the water that I shall give him will become in him a fountain of water springing up into everlasting life,"* (John 4:13-14). *"On the last day, that great day of the feast, Jesus stood and cried out, saying, 'If anyone thirsts, let him come to Me and drink,'"* (John 7:37). The water spoken of here is the water of *life*, spiritual, eternal *life*. Life only comes from God, therefore this water we will be drinking is **life** that comes from or through our Creator flowing from His throne and the throne of the Lamb.

In the middle of its street and on either side of the river is the tree of life, which bore twelve fruits, each tree yielding its fruit every month. The leaves of the tree are for the healing of the nations. God has, *'made all things new'* so exactly how the nations are healed and what the fruit is we can only imagine. Also, it seems that a twelve month year will be part of the new heaven and earth which indicates there will be some means of measuring time without the sun or the moon.

The leaves will be for the healing of the nations, indicating the continued spiritually healthy state we will enjoy for all eternity because of the presence of our Lord. The curse which God pronounced in Gen.3:17 will have been lifted and everything associated with

the curse will also have been removed, and we will
serve Him continually. We will see His face and have
His Name written on our forehead: "Belonging to
Yahweh."

In the first creation, there was night and day; in the
new creation there will be no more night, nor getting
tired, nor need to sleep. The light of the new heaven
and earth is God Himself, there will be no need of the
sun and moon.

Vs.6-11: *"Then he said to me, "These words are
faithful and true." And the Lord God of the holy
prophets sent His angel to show His servants the things
which must shortly take place. "Behold, I am coming
quickly! Blessed is he who keeps the words of the
prophecy of this book." Now I, John, saw and heard
these things. And when I heard and saw, I fell down
to worship before the feet of the angel who showed
me these things. Then he said to me, "See that you
do not do that. For I am your fellow servant, and of
your brethren the prophets, and of those who keep the
words of this book. Worship God." And he said to me,
"Do not seal the words of the prophecy of this book,
for the time is at hand. He who is unjust, let him be
unjust still; he who is filthy, let him be filthy still; he
who is righteous, let him be righteous still; he who is
holy, let him be holy still."*

John is assured that all he has been shown, "these
words," are both real and true. It will come to pass

just as he's been shown. John has been shown ultimate reality, the risen and glorified Jesus. Sometimes with things such as they are in the world we ask one another, "I wonder what all this is going to come to"? If we read and study the great book of Revelation we actually know the answer. Here we have been shown in no uncertain terms where the world is heading and that disclosure is very sobering. As he was told in Rev.1:1 John is reminded that these things are going to take place shortly. When we think that John received the revelation about 2,000 years ago we realize how close we are to the rapture of the Church. Again John is reminded that there is a blessing promised to those who keep the words of the prophecy of this book. The word for "this book" used here is *Bib-lee-on,* which would seem to indicate the entire Bible not just Revelation.

In verses 8 and 9 we wonder if John had mistaken the angel for Jesus because he bows down to worship him but is quickly corrected. This same thing occurred back in chapter 19:10 and John is told, "WORSHIP GOD." Song writer Bob Dylan professed faith in Christ for a short while and on his album <u>Slow Train Coming</u> one of the songs is, *You're Gonna Serve Somebody.* The lyrics make a very powerful point that regardless of your position, station, or situation in life, *Still, you're gonna have to serve somebody, yes you're gonna have to serve somebody; Well, it may be the devil or it may be the Lord but you're gonna have to serve somebody."* Everybody is serving somebody whether they admit it or not. John is told here and we are told here, worship God; the One, True, Living God as he has revealed Himself in His word. Sadly, there are those who have created their own custom made god whom they have fashioned to fit what suites them. This way they don't ever have to be inconvenienced or feel uncomfortable by allowing God's Word to expose to them their true hearts and true motives. *"For the word of God is living and powerful, and sharper than any two-edged sword, piercing even to the division of soul and spirit, and of joints and marrow, and is a discerner of the thoughts and intents of the heart. And there is no creature hidden from His sight, but all things are naked and open to the eyes of Him to whom we must give account,"* (Heb 4:12-13).

In verse 10, John is instructed specifically not to seal the prophecy of this book – the opposite of what he was told regarding the voice of the seven thunders. I believe he's told not to seal them because these things are about to happen shortly. I believe verse 11 is simply telling the reader to be what they want to be, but don't expect the reward for other than what they have chosen. Many want to live for the world and still receive the reward of heaven, but that won't happen. This has been the very clear message from the beginning, *choose.* There's no such thing as straddling the fence when it comes to spiritual matters, because God has given us His word. There is no neutral ground when it comes to God. We can choose to read it and take it into our heart and mind, or we can choose to disregard and ignore it. It's our own choice. I love how Joshua put it, *"And if it seems evil to you to serve the Lord, choose for yourselves this day whom you will serve, whether the gods which your fathers served that were on the other side of the River, or the gods of the Amorites, in whose land you dwell. But as for me and my house, we will serve the Lord,"* (Joshua 24:15).

Revelation's conclusion:

Vs.12-21: *"And behold, I am coming quickly, and My reward is with Me, to give to every one according to his work. I am the Alpha and the Omega, the Beginning and the End, the First and the Last. Blessed are those who do His commandments, that they may have the right to the tree of life, and may enter through the gates into the city. But outside are dogs and sorcerers and sexually immoral and murderers and idolaters, and whoever loves and practices a lie. I, Jesus, have sent My angel to testify to you these things in the churches. I am the Root and the Offspring of David, the Bright and Morning Star. And the Spirit and the bride say, "Come!" And let him who hears say, "Come!" And let him who thirsts come. Whoever desires, let him take the water of life freely. For I testify to everyone who hears the words of the prophecy of this book: If anyone adds to these things, God will add to him the plagues that are written in this book; and if anyone takes away from the words of the book of this prophecy, God shall take away his part from the Book of Life, from the holy city, and from the things which are written in this book. I Am Coming Quickly He who testifies to these things says, "Surely I am coming quickly." Amen. Even so, come, Lord Jesus! The grace of our Lord Jesus Christ be with you all. Amen."*

This last portion concludes everything this book of prophecy has instructed us about. Notice it does not tell us that Jesus is coming *soon*, but that He is coming quickly. Therefore, we are to live as Christians, not people of the world. This book is testified by Jesus Himself to be true; anyone who adds or removes from this book will be removed from the book of life because to do so would be to call Jesus a liar. Deut.4:2; Isa. 40:8 and Prov.30:5,6 also issue a strong warning against changing any part of God's word.

Think of how great God is. We cannot stretch our minds to comprehend His greatness nor His goodness. How profoundly tragic is it that millions of people follow, with ardent devotion and unquestioned obedience, their false gods who neither love them nor provide for them. The challenge of Rom. 10:14 comes to mind, *"How then shall they call on Him in whom they have not believed? And how shall they believe in Him of whom they have not heard? And how shall they hear without a preacher?"* as well as 2 Cor 5:11, *"Knowing, therefore, the terror of the Lord, we persuade men."* Our great and loving God planned the way of salvation for all men before the foundation of the world. And then, He sent His only Son to be the atoning sacrifice for our sin at a time when we were, *"Aliens from the commonwealth of Israel and strangers from the covenants of promise, having no hope and without God in the world. But now in Christ Jesus you who once were far off have been brought near by the blood of Christ,"* (Eph 2:12-13). *"But God demonstrates His own love toward us, in that while we were still sinners, Christ died for us,"* (Rom 5:8). So our God brings salvation by the new birth and then He makes known to us, by illumination of His Holy Spirit, His Word and His plan down through the ages right up to the end of the age. The great book of Revelation was meant to be a book of hope for all believers through the ages. Therefore, as believers let's pray that our lives echo the cry of verse 20, *"Even so, come quickly Lord Jesus!"*

WORKS CITED

Biblestudytools.com (Aug. 2019)

Jerome Smith, The New Treasury of Scripture Knowledge 1992 (Jan. 2019)

Knapton, Sarah. "Aborted Babies Incinerated to Heat UK Hospitals." *The Telegraph*, Telegraph Media Group, 15 Mar. 2016, www.telegraph.co.uk/science/2016/03/15/aborted-babies-incinerated-to-heat-uk-hospitals/. (Sept.2017)

Moisse, Katie. "Bill Would Ban Aborted Fetuses in Food." *ABC News*, ABC News Network, 26 Jan. 2012, abcnews.go.com/blogs/health/2012/01/26/bill-would-ban-aborted-fetuses-in-food/. (Sept. 2017)

New Unger's Bible Dictionary (July 2018)

Strong's Greek Hebrew Definitions #3354

The Vatican Billions by Avro Mahattan ISBN #0937958166

CPSIA information can be obtained
at www.ICGtesting.com
Printed in the USA
LVHW082318200721
693264LV00013B/749

9 781973 687245